Praise for *The Year of Mourning*

Grief is a universal human experience; it stimulates spiritual reflection and yearns for a communal response. Rabbi Lisa D. Grant and Cantor Lisa B. Segal have planted important flora on the inevitable path of grief that we all walk. Each page is a place to linger, look, listen, and reflect. Whether this book sits on your lap or you scroll through it on your device, anywhere your eye focuses will bring a moment of nourishment on your journey.

—RABBI ERIC WEISS
editor of *Mishkan Aveilut: Where Grief Resides*

The Year of Mourning is a must-have for every clergyperson. After nearly thirty years of guiding congregants through the grieving process, I finally have an all-in-one resource to offer comfort and support beyond the funeral and shivah. Understanding that everyone grieves differently, the editors have created a collection of individual units that gives mourners the ability to move through at their own pace. This special compilation of music, poetry, and reflective questions is a wonderful resource.

—CANTOR CLAIRE FRANCO
Past-President, American Conference of Cantors

The Year of MOURNING

The Year of MOURNING

A Jewish Journey

EDITOR
Rabbi Lisa D. Grant, PhD

CONSULTING EDITOR
Cantor Lisa B. Segal

FOREWORD BY
Rabbi Richard F. Address, DMin

CCAR PRESS
CENTRAL CONFERENCE OF AMERICAN RABBIS
5783 New York 2023

LIBRARY OF CONGRESS CATALOGING-IN-PUBLICATION DATA
Names: Grant, Lisa D., editor. | Segal, Lisa B., editor.
Title: The year of mourning: a Jewish journey / Lisa D. Grant, Lisa B. Segal.
Description: New York: Central Conference of American Rabbis (CCAR), 2022. | Includes bibliographical references. | Summary: "Offers an expansive array of resources—stories, songs, study texts, poetry, and prayers—to guide the bereaved through the first year after their loss. Each week the mourner is encouraged to focus on a particular theme to deepen their Kaddish practice. The book also includes new rituals for shivah, sh'loshim, unveiling, and yahrzeit"—Provided by publisher.
Identifiers: LCCN 2021052876 (print) | LCCN 2021052877 (ebook) | ISBN 9780881236071 (trade paperback) | ISBN 9780881236088 (ebook)
Subjects: LCSH: Jewish mourning customs. | Jewish funeral rites and ceremonies. | Death—Religious aspects—Judaism.
Classification: LCC BM712 .Y43 2022 (print) | LCC BM712 (ebook) | DDC 296.4/45—dc23/eng/20211208
LC record available at https://lccn.loc.gov/2021052876
LC ebook record available at https://lccn.loc.gov/2021052877

Book and cover design by Scott-Martin Kosofsky
at The Philidor Company, Rhinebeck, NY

Cover art: *By Sleep*, 2020, © Audrey Stone.
Used by permission of the artist.

10 9 8 7 6 5 4 3 2 1 0

Published by CCAR Press
Central Conference of American Rabbis
355 Lexington Avenue, New York, NY 10017
(212) 972-3636 | info@ccarpress.org
www.ccarpress.org

In memory of
Rabbi A. Stanley Dreyfus
and Marianne C. Dreyfus,
whose dedication to the memory
of their forebears
is an enduring lesson
to their descendants.

Their memory is a blessing
to all who knew them.

Contents

Foreword: Why Now? Why Not? Mourning's Winding Road xi
Rabbi Richard F. Address, DMin

Acknowledgments xv

Cover Artist's Statement xvii

Introduction xix

Check-Ins: Being There for Yourself xxiii

Pain: I Have Lost You Forever 1

Brokenness: You Were Taken from Me Too Early 21

Sadness: How Can I Live without You? 43

Comfort: Seeking Support 65

Resilience: How I Can Still Feel Close to You 85

Acceptance: Honoring You, Honoring Myself 107

Gratitude: Living with Your Memory 129

Group Rituals 151

A Ritual for after the Funeral: Beginning to Sit Shivah 153

A Ritual to Mark the End of Shivah 158

A Ritual to Mark the End of *Sh'loshim* 163

Matzeivah (Unveiling of the Tombstone): A Ritual for Revisiting 167

Marking the *Yahrzeit*: A Ritual of Transitioning 170

Kaddish and Mourning Prayers 175

Resources 177

Sources and Permissions 179

About the Editors 187

FOREWORD

Why Now? Why Not? Mourning's Winding Road

Rabbi Richard F. Address, DMin

In recent years, COVID-19 has impacted every aspect of life and death. The long-term implications of virtual funerals and shivah gatherings and the reality of delayed mourning will be part of who we are for years to come. Without the "due process" of familiar rituals, many of our people will hold on to emotions. We know that the need for these rituals is fundamental to who we are as human beings.

With *The Year of Mourning: A Jewish Journey*, we are being invited to reimagine what some of the aspects of our individual journey may be. We know that there is no template for the journey, that each of us travels this road in our own unique way, bringing our own personal, as well as family of origin, imprints to bear. Mourning is personal, and the prayers, melodies, meditations, and rituals become the scaffolding that makes it possible for our souls to be rebuilt.

These tools allow us to make sense out of time in a time when we feel disoriented. They help weave a fabric of meaning that permits us to find shelter from life's randomness. As Dr. Lawrence A. Hoffman has written, "Ritual helps us minimize our dependence on chance. It arranges our life into relatively small packages of moments that matter" (*The Art of Public Prayer*, p. 17). Dr. Kenneth I. Pargament echoes Hoffman in writing that "rituals can be understood, in part, as methods to reduce anxiety, create meaning in life, encourage emotional expression and emotional control, foster personal identity, and promote group cohesiveness" (*Spiritually Integrated Psychotherapy*, p. 81).

The pandemic has sparked a powerful creative wave of new modalities associated with the journey through mourning. This wave of creativity will remain with us long after the pandemic subsides. The basic human desires for relationships and connection, and for meaning out of chaos and randomness, have been a driving force in this creative rush. We have sought more personal expressions of what it means to navigate mourning's journey. A growing cadre of rabbis, cantors, educators, and liturgists have supported this more egalitarian and inclusive movement. All this has produced powerful and inspirational expressions of self and soul, many of which are contained here.

If, as Heschel says, we are creatures in search of meaning, then there may be no greater moment when meaning becomes front and center than in the face of and aftermath of death. Psalm 23's *tzalmavet*, "shadow of death," hangs over us throughout our life. The reality of our own mortality helps shape who we are, how we live, and even how we face death. It is the reality of Genesis 3—the expulsion from Eden and the beginning of human mortality—and the confrontation of our desire to live coming face-to-face with the truth that we eventually will die, that has driven the births of entire civilizations and religions. We seek to create rituals, traditions, symbols that give us, we hope, a sense of what a life can mean. The acceptance of our own mortality, as Rabbi Grant reminds us, is a major step in our own spiritual growth. This acceptance is reflected in the following from a veteran chaplain, himself confronting the reality of his own mortality: "We don't have to like the reality of being human. But once we begin to accept our own humanity with some humility, we can then deal with hope, within the natural order of the world" (Rafael Goldstein, *Psalms in the Key of Healing*, p. 82).

Ultimately, our Jewish rituals and prayers are about that sense of hope. We get up at the end of shivah and take a small walk symbolizing our "return." No one takes that walk unscathed. Like Jacob's wound in Genesis 32, we carry the loss with us, but as our tradition teaches and models, we emerge from shivah, we pray, infused with the power of memory and with hope that this memory can serve as a source of blessing and inspiration. Our rituals and prayers allow for this memory to become a marker in our own life's journey, a part of who we are.

In the morning service we read a wonderful prayer, the *Eilu D'varim*, which speaks of the things that we must do as a Jew. One of these mitzvot is *l'vayat hameit*, "accompanying the dead." This is a beautiful image for us, for in the mourning process we accompany the dead through the rituals leading to burial. However, equally valuable is the fact that the rituals allow us to move through our own stages of grief. Rabbi Lisa D. Grant's seven steps or stages can be viewed as steps that can accompany us on our journeys of mourning. Additionally, they encourage us to build a support system. Community is being reimagined, since at the heart of this remains the basic desire, in each of us, for human contact and for the embrace of friends and family.

Another aspect of our journey through mourning is the tension of holding on and letting go. A death changes things. The Jewish rituals associated with death and mourning aid in the understanding that time is an essential element of our journey. As we mentioned, there is no set timetable for this. Each of us traverses this wilderness in our own way. There is a gradual tension between us trying to hold on to a life and the reality that we have to let go of the physical manifestation of that life. Dr. Daniel Gottlieb, a therapist, speaks to the value of shivah as a pathway: "How do we let go of the things that are so precious to us? And there are many of those things. . . . We let go through tears and sadness and fear and grief. But for most of us, tears don't happen until we let down, exhale, and open up to the truth of our lives" (*The Wisdom We're Born With*, p. 87).

That truth often emerges in slow and quiet ways as we make this journey through mourning. It is a truth that lies at the heart of each of us; it is the most fundamental need of every human being. It is the truth of our fundamental need for love, to be loved and to love. To make the journey through mourning is to be tested on how we transition the love we have for another from a physical sense to a spiritual one, a move that takes time and for which our faith tradition offers guidance, support, and care. The power of memory ensures that the love will remain within our souls, serving, we pray, as a source of inspiration and blessing. Or, to put it more simply, as Mitch Albom wrote in his classic *Tuesdays with Morrie*, "Death ends a life, not a relationship" (p. 174).

Rabbi Richard F. Address, DMin, is the founder and director of the Jewish Sacred Aging forum (www.jewishsacredaging.com). Rabbi Address served for over three decades on staff for the Union for Reform Judaism, first as a regional director and then as the founder and director of the URJ's Department of Jewish Family Concerns. He was ordained from Hebrew Union College–Jewish Institute of Religion in 1972 and has served congregations in Los Angeles and New Jersey.

Acknowledgments

Many people provided inspiration, support, guidance, and wisdom in the creation of these materials. First and foremost, Rabbi Lisa D. Grant, PhD, wants to thank her creative partner, Cantor Lisa B. Segal, whose knowledge and love of Jewish sacred music and whose sweet voice infuses every aspect of this project. Cantor Lisa B. Segal is grateful to her friend and colleague, Rabbi Lisa D. Grant, PhD, for drawing her into this project, her instinct for finding the right texts for each moment, and for her partnership in making the musical choices.

We both are most grateful to Rabbi Sonja K. Pilz, PhD, who played an invaluable role as editor extraordinaire and patient shepherd as we shaped, reshaped, expanded upon, and enriched the initial material to better fit with this multimedia presentation. We also thank Rabbi Jan Katz, who took over from Rabbi Pilz to guide the project through its final months of production. Additionally, we are so grateful for the contributions of all the poets and sacred musicians represented here—many of whom are friends, all of whom are inspirational teachers. We are grateful for being in community with longtime Kolot Chayeinu member Audrey Stone, whose gorgeous and moving work graces the cover of this volume. Special thanks to Cantor Josh Breitzer for his insights and support, and to Michelle Citrin, whose ear and belief in the power of music made producing Cantor Segal's tracks a brilliant joy.

Thank you to Rabbi Hara Person for imagining what this collection of resources could become and having the faith in us to create it. Thank you too to dear friends and colleagues Merri Lovinger Arian, Andrew Feinstein, Beth Girshman, David Kasakove, and Rabbi Ellen Lippmann, who shared resources that they found brought them some modicum of comfort when they mourned.

The CCAR Editorial Committee for this project provided helpful feedback and creative suggestions. We are grateful to the rest of the Press staff, Rafael Chaiken, Debbie Smilow, Raquel Fairweather-Gallie, and Chiara Ricisak. We also want to express our gratitude for the hard work of copy editor Debra Corman, proofreader Michelle Kwitkin, and designer Scott-Martin Kosofsky in transforming the manuscript into a book.

Rabbi Grant dedicates this work to her parents, Murray J. Grant, *z"l*, יחיאל משה בן רפאל הכהן ולאה, and Marilyn Ruth Grant, *z"l*, מרים רות בת פייבל וצילה.

Cantor Segal dedicates the work to her Kolot Chayeinu congregants and the memories of their loved ones, to her *zayde* Roy/Reuven Abrams, *z"l*, her wonderful stepfather Roland Lee Minda, *z"l*, and her sweet father, Howard "Howie" Segal, *z"l*, whose memories and music live inside her.

Their memories are a constant presence in our lives and show that as long as we are able to remember, our loved ones are never fully lost to us.

Cover Artist's Statement

Audrey Stone

"By Sleep," 2020, is one of eighteen paintings I created between 2019 and 2020 during and after my experience of multiple personal losses. (Eighteen is the numerical value of *chai*, the Hebrew word for "life," so while the series is about death, it is also about the living.) The series title, "By Fire," refers to Leonard Cohen's song "Who by Fire"; the individual painting titles refer to lines in Cohen's song, to the *Un'taneh Tokef* prayer from the High Holy Days that inspired it, and to my own interpretive riffs on both. I produced the series in something of a cathartic fury while deeply in mourning, constantly immersed in the song and the prayer. They are all vertical, like portraits, and ideally all eighteen would be seen together; taken individually each one confronts a particular way of dying and the mystery that surrounds that transition. When I came to paint "By Sleep," I remembered thinking as a child that dying in one's sleep would be the ideal, and then later learning about people I knew who did so. When I conceived this piece I was contemplating the moments between sleep (the settled darkness at the bottom of the painting) and wakefulness (the rising light above)—and the gentle slipping of consciousness between the two that some liken to surfing. My experience of grief has been that while it never truly ends, it does ebb and flow and change as time passes. The painting's gradient of color—without a definitive ending—suggests a quiet passage from sleep into death, as well as the gradual transformation of the lives of those left behind: the almost immeasurable shifts and transitions as one moves through grief, perhaps eventually arriving at transcendence.

Introduction

Rabbi Lisa D. Grant, PhD

THIS PROJECT grew out of a personal need. For several weeks following my mother's death in December 2014, a cluster of deaths occurred in my synagogue community. Similarly, at Hebrew Union College–Jewish Institute of Religion, New York, where I teach, a sizable group of students and colleagues were mourning the deaths of parents around this same time. I felt blessed to have this community of fellow mourners at school, which made me think about how to bring together the mourners in my congregation to provide some extra support during this time of vulnerability and grief, building community at the same time. So, I began a "*Kaddish* club," inviting anyone who had experienced the death of a loved one in recent months to come.

The group met monthly over many months. Participation in the group was fluid, ranging between six and ten participants each time. Individuals were mourning partners and spouses, parents, children, friends, and other relatives. Participants ranged in age from thirty to over seventy. We met at my home or the home of another mourner and would share a meal as part of our gathering.

Each month, we would study a text relating to Jewish mourning practices and grief. Sometimes the topics came from me, and other times they grew out of the conversations and questions that arose from the prior gathering. In addition to study, we told stories about our loved ones. We sang together and concluded each session by reciting the Mourner's *Kaddish*.

What I saw in these mourners was a need to be in safe spaces to share their stories, to commune in their grief, and to find solace in the comfort of others. I also saw curiosity, the desire to know more about what Jewish tradition can teach about mourning practices, and a willingness to explore how traditional wisdom and practices might support them in their personal journey through grief. The motivations, stories, and curiosity of these learners were with me as I began to shape the journey on which you will go with this book.

Cantor Lisa B. Segal

In *Man's Quest for God*, Rabbi Abraham Joshua Heschel wrote that there are three ways to mourn: first to cry, then to grow silent, and third to transform sorrow into song.

I often begin a funeral or shiva minyan with a *nigun*, because a *nigun* comes from a place beyond words, the realm of the ineffable. Texts, be they traditional liturgy, interpretation, or poetic original lyrics, can resonate, inspiring emotion, memory, and insight.

As Rabbi Grant and I approached the musical choices for this project, we searched for musical expression in melody, rhythm, tone, and text that speak to each theme in the book. While not every offering will speak to you, our hope is that many will.

In the midst of recording music for this project, my wonderful father died, and at this writing I am finding my own path through the Kaddish year, experiencing keenly the need for these texts and songs. I hope that my voice and that of other sacred musicians will touch you in that place beyond language, helping transform sorrow into song.

This Book

The year of mourning is often a time of disorientation and disruption. After experiencing the death of a loved one, people yearn for the comfort of home but often find it ruptured and inhospitable. During this period of disequilibrium, many find they do not have the inner resources to go it alone. It is a time when people often look to outside sources for wisdom, support, comfort, and realignment. Jewish learning and Jewish community can be especially powerful sources of support when people are at their most vulnerable. This guided journey is offered as a resource to support individuals regain their grounding after loss, as a way to return home with deepened connections to memories of loved ones, to the richness of Jewish tradition, and to others in their community who may be walking along a similar path.

This compilation of resources is organized around seven metathemes, each of which includes seven separate units:

1. Pain: I have lost you forever.
2. Brokenness: You were taken from me too early.
3. Sadness: How can I live without you?

4. Comfort: Seeking support.
5. Resilience: How I can still feel close to you.
6. Acceptance: Honoring you, honoring myself.
7. Gratitude: Living with your memory.

Each of the units begins with a song and then a *kavanah*, a way to check in with yourself and set an intention for exploring the material to follow. This opening question is followed by a text with guiding questions for study, poetry, and prayer—all of which relate in some way to the theme. Each unit also offers the mourner the opportunity to recite the Mourner's *Kaddish* and listen to a brief chant of remembrance.

Just as mourning does not follow a predictable path, so, too, can the themes and individual units within them be seen as having more of a circular rather than linear progression. There is no intention to prescribe a set sequence. Some may choose to go in order, and others may seek out a theme or a text or a song that connects most deeply to their experience in each particular moment.

We take note that a number of songs are offered more than once, appearing in multiple units, as their texts and themes speak to different experiences.

In addition to these forty-nine units that can be explored at your own pace and in your own pattern, there are five group rituals that are linked to specific moments in the cycle of mourning. These rituals are designed to be done at home and can include other family members and friends. They mark the following moments:

1. After the funeral
2. The end of the first thirty days
3. Around the midpoint of the year
4. A ceremony of unveiling a grave marker
5. The first *yahrzeit*/anniversary of your loved one's death

The Year of Mourning is available as both a book and a digital app. The app includes recordings of the songs, weekly reminders, ways to track your progress, and more. If you do not have access to the app, many of the songs can be found by searching on Spotify or YouTube.

May these resources bring you closer to wholeness and healing as you journey throughout the year.

בָּרוּךְ אַתָּה, יְיָ, מְנַחֵם לֵב אֲבֵלִים.

Baruch atah, Adonai, m'nacheim lev aveilim.

Blessed is the Holy One, who comforts the hearts of mourners.

Check-Ins: Being There for Yourself

Themes

1. Pain: I have lost you forever.
2. Brokenness: You were taken from me too early.
3. Sadness: How can I live without you?
4. Comfort: Seeking support.
5. Resilience: How I can still feel close to you.
6. Acceptance: Honoring you, honoring myself.
7. Gratitude: Living with your memory.

Song

For each check-in with yourself and for each group ritual, you may decide to open with a song. Many of the song texts come from the Book of Psalms, while others include medieval Hebrew poetry and contemporary compositions. Music and singing can helps us to feel more present. It may prepare us for whatever we decide to do next, grounding us and offering a contemplative opening. As you find songs that speak to you, we invite you to listen again and again, to follow the texts, to sing along.

Kavanah

This section invites reflection through writing a journal entry. If you are checking in by yourself, you can use this time to write about a memory of the person you are mourning. If you are checking in with friends and family, everyone can share memories of the person you are mourning together.

Sacred Sources

Each session provides a sacred text or a group of related texts. You may choose to simply immerse yourself: read the words of Jewish tradition and wisdom. Or you may choose to read through the guiding questions provided to help you explore the deeper meaning of those texts and relate them to your own personal experiences of mourning.

Poetry and Prayer

Modern poems and prayers give words to the feelings, needs, hopes, and challenges you might not have been able to verbalize yourself.

Kaddish and Mourning Prayers

You may choose to end your check-in or group session by reciting the Mourner's *Kaddish* and/or chanting a mourning prayer.

PAIN

I Have Lost You Forever

Week 1

Song

Psalm 23: *Adonai Ro-i*
Text: Psalm 23
Music: Hazzan Max Wohlberg

מִזְמוֹר לְדָוִד:
יְיָ רֹעִי, לֹא אֶחְסָר.
בִּנְאוֹת דֶּשֶׁא יַרְבִּיצֵנִי עַל מֵי מְנֻחוֹת יְנַהֲלֵנִי.
נַפְשִׁי יְשׁוֹבֵב יַנְחֵנִי בְמַעְגְּלֵי צֶדֶק לְמַעַן שְׁמוֹ.
גַּם כִּי אֵלֵךְ בְּגֵיא צַלְמָוֶת לֹא אִירָא רָע כִּי אַתָּה עִמָּדִי.
שִׁבְטְךָ וּמִשְׁעַנְתֶּךָ הֵמָּה יְנַחֲמֻנִי.
תַּעֲרֹךְ לְפָנַי שֻׁלְחָן נֶגֶד צֹרְרָי.
דִּשַּׁנְתָּ בַשֶּׁמֶן רֹאשִׁי כּוֹסִי רְוָיָה.
אַךְ טוֹב וָחֶסֶד יִרְדְּפוּנִי כָּל יְמֵי חַיָּי.
וְשַׁבְתִּי בְּבֵית יְיָ לְאֹרֶךְ יָמִים.

A Psalm of David.
Adonai is my shepherd, I am complete.
In lush meadows You let me lie down.
Alongside tranquil waters You lead me.
You restore my life.
You guide me in paths of righteousness for the sake of Your name.
Even when I walk through the valley of deep darkness,
I fear no harm, for You are with me.
Your rod and Your staff, they reassure me.
You set a table before me in the presence of my enemies.
You anoint my head with oil; wine brims over my cup.
Indeed, goodness and steadfast love shall pursue me all the days of my life;
And I shall dwell in the house of Adonai as long as I live.

Kavanah

In the first days after the death of a beloved one, we are often numb to pain—only to be overwhelmed and paralyzed by it at other times. As we are thrown back and forth between forgetful distraction and sudden, painful moments of realization, we find our inner selves looking for words, trying to grasp the ungraspable.

Take a moment. Just breathe. Remember the face of your loved one. Hold it tight.

Sacred Sources

> Then Jacob tore his clothes, put sackcloth on his loins, and mourned his son many days. His sons and daughters endeavored to console him, but he refused to be consoled, saying, "No, in mourning shall I go down to my son to Sheol!" Thus did his father bewail him. (Genesis 37:34–35)

- How would you describe the emotions that overcome Jacob upon hearing about the death of his beloved son Joseph?
- How do the people surrounding Jacob react to his mourning? What might motivate them to try to console him?
- Imagine yourself sitting next to Jacob. How would you react to his pain? In what way could you show the same empathy to yourself?

Poetry and Prayer

In Sorrow
Alden Solovy

Ancient One,
Send light into this darkness
And hope into this despair.
Send music into this emptiness
And healing into this aching heart.

Air.
All I need is air.
A breath to give oxygen
To the anguish within.

A breath to give voice
To the howl in my heart.
A breath to set me free.

I am undone.
Crushed silent by sorrow.
Bereft by loneliness and loss.
Still yearning for healing.
Still yearning for love.
Still yearning for You.

Ancient One,
Send light into this darkness
And hope into this despair.
Send music into this emptiness
And healing into this aching heart.

Kaddish and Mourning Prayers

See page 175.

Week 2

Song

Bishvili Nivra HaOlam
Text: Babylonian Talmud, *Sanhedrin* 37a; Genesis 18:27
Music: Julie Geller

בִּשְׁבִילִי נִבְרָא הָעוֹלָם
וְאָנֹכִי עָפָר וָאֵפֶר.

Bishvili nivra haolam,
v'anochi afar va-eifer.

The world was created for me [Babylonian Talmud, *Sanhedrin* 37a],
I am dust and ashes [Genesis 18:27].

Kavanah

Sometimes, we might find our breathing stops as we realize that we will never be able to ask another question; to say "I love you"; to give a hug; to share a story about ourselves; to talk to the one we have lost, ever again . . . Realizing that some opportunities might be missed forever, we feel a sharp pain settling into our chest.

Take the time. Find the words—inside you, on paper, or in the words of someone else. Let them sink in. Speak them. Share them with others.

Sacred Sources

Rabbi Akiva was not present at the time of his teacher Rabbi Eliezer's death. At the conclusion of Shabbat, Rabbi Akiva encountered the funeral procession on his way from Caesarea to Lod. Rabbi Akiva was striking his flesh in terrible anguish and regret until his blood flowed to the earth. He began to eulogize Rabbi Eliezer in the row of those comforting the mourners, and said, "My father, my father, the chariot of Israel and its horsemen [2 Kings 2:12]. I have many coins, but I do not have a money changer to whom to give them; I have many questions, but after your death I have no one who can answer them." (Babylonian Talmud, *Sanhedrin* 68a)

- We read that Rabbi Akiva was striking his flesh when he heard about the surprising death of a beloved teacher with whom he had a complicated relationship. How do feelings of remorse over things that remain unsaid and undone impact us?
- Rabbi Akiva finds names that express his deep love and honor for the deceased. Which names can you find for the loved one you lost to express what they meant to you?
- Sometimes, we might find ourselves drowning in pain, or, as the Talmud puts it, we might see our "blood flowing to the earth." Has there been a moment when your own "blood and tears" flowed to the earth? See if you can write it down or talk about that experience.

Poetry and Prayer

Because We Spill Not Only Milk

Nancy Schaffer

Because we spill not only milk
knocking it over with an elbow
when we reach to wipe a small face
but also spill seed on soil we
thought was fertile but isn't
and also spill whole lives, and only
later see in fading light how
much is gone and we hadn't
intended it

Because we tear not only cloth
thinking to find a true edge and
instead making only a hole but
also tear friendships when we grow
and whole mountainsides
because we are so many and
we want to live right where black oaks
lived, once very quietly and still

Because we forget not only what
we are doing in the kitchen

and have to go back to the room we were in
before, remember why it was we left
but also forget entire lexicons of joy and
how we lost ourselves for hours
yet all that time were clearly
found and held and also forget
the hungry not at our table

Because we weep not only at jade
plants caught in freeze and
precious papers left in rain but
also at legs that no longer walk
or never did, although from the outside
they look like most others
and also weep at words said once as
though they might be rearranged but
which, once loose, refuse to return
and we are helpless

Because we are imperfect and love so
deeply we will never have enough days
we need the gift of starting over, beginning
again: just this constant good, this
saving hope.

Kaddish and Mourning Prayers

See page 175.

Week 3

Song

Oseh Shalom
Text: *Amidah*
Music: Robert Weinberg

עֹשֶׂה שָׁלוֹם בִּמְרוֹמָיו, הוּא יַעֲשֶׂה שָׁלוֹם עָלֵינוּ
וְעַל כָּל יִשְׂרָאֵל, וְאִמְרוּ: אָמֵן.

Oseh shalom bimromav, hu yaaseh shalom aleinu
v'al kol Yisrael, v'imru: Amen.

May the One who brings peace in the heavens, bring peace for us and for all Israel [and for all humankind], and let us say: *Amen*.

Kavanah

The practice of tearing garments just before burying a loved one can be traced back to the Talmud, where detailed instructions are provided about what and how to tear and who should partake in this custom. In liberal Jewish communities, most mourners tear a black ribbon that they wear (often throughout the period of shivah) as a symbol of the rupture that takes place when a loved one dies. And yet, we know that the feeling of rupture does not end after a week. It may linger for a long time.

Where in your body do you feel torn apart by the death of your loved one? Has this feeling changed at all for you?

Sacred Sources

With regard to all other deceased relatives, one tears a garment the length of a handbreadth, and that suffices. In the case of a father or mother, one must tear until the heart is exposed. . . . With regard to all other deceased relatives, even if one is wearing ten garments, one tears only the outer garment. For one's father or mother, one must rend them all. And one's undergarment is not indispensable either for a man or woman. . . . And Rabbi Chiya bar Abba said that Rabbi Yochanan said: For all dead, one may tear using a tool or by hand; for one's father or mother only by hand. For all dead, one tears indoors, but for one's mother or father, one tears in public. (Babylonian Talmud, *Mo-eid Katan* 22b)

Any tear that a person makes over a relative other than parents can be basted after seven days and repaired after thirty days. For one's father and mother, one can baste after thirty days, but never repair. . . . Just as one must tear for one's father and mother, so one is obligated to tear for one's teacher who taught one Torah, for the patriarch of the community, and for the chief of the court, and for a large part of the community that has been slain for the cursing of God's name, for the burning of a Torah scroll, and when seeing the cities of Judah, Jerusalem, and the Temple in ruins. (Maimonides, *Mishneh Torah, Laws of Mourning* 9:1–2)

- Why do you think the Rabbis differentiated the practices for tearing for a parent from other deceased relatives and loved ones?
- What values do you think these distinctions express?
- Why do you think the tear for a parent can never be repaired? What kind of tear does this represent? How is it different from a tear for the death of a spouse or a child, either of which might cause even greater pain and suffering than the death of a parent?

Poetry and Prayer

Tearing

Rivka Miriam, translated by Rabbi Steven Sager

There was a peaceful tearing
like the peaceful tearing of twilight
when the warp and woof are parted for an instant
so that their continuing can take place
like the tearing that parts the eyelids
in the morning
when sleep dissolves before wakefulness rises to a new beginning.

Kaddish and Mourning Prayers

See page 175.

Week 4

Song

Psalm 23: *Adonai Ro-i*
Text: Psalm 23
Music: Hazzan Max Wohlberg

מִזְמוֹר לְדָוִד:
יְיָ רֹעִי, לֹא אֶחְסָר.
בִּנְאוֹת דֶּשֶׁא יַרְבִּיצֵנִי עַל מֵי מְנֻחוֹת יְנַהֲלֵנִי.
נַפְשִׁי יְשׁוֹבֵב יַנְחֵנִי בְמַעְגְּלֵי צֶדֶק לְמַעַן שְׁמוֹ.
גַּם כִּי אֵלֵךְ בְּגֵיא צַלְמָוֶת לֹא אִירָא רָע כִּי אַתָּה עִמָּדִי.
שִׁבְטְךָ וּמִשְׁעַנְתֶּךָ הֵמָּה יְנַחֲמֻנִי.
תַּעֲרֹךְ לְפָנַי שֻׁלְחָן נֶגֶד צֹרְרָי.
דִּשַּׁנְתָּ בַשֶּׁמֶן רֹאשִׁי כּוֹסִי רְוָיָה.
אַךְ טוֹב וָחֶסֶד יִרְדְּפוּנִי כָּל יְמֵי חַיָּי.
וְשַׁבְתִּי בְּבֵית יְיָ לְאֹרֶךְ יָמִים.

A Psalm of David.
Adonai is my shepherd, I am complete.
In lush meadows You let me lie down.
Alongside tranquil waters You lead me.
You restore my life.
You guide me in paths of righteousness for the sake of Your name.
Even when I walk through the valley of deep darkness,
I fear no harm, for You are with me.
Your rod and Your staff, they reassure me.
You set a table before me in the presence of my enemies.
You anoint my head with oil; wine brims over my cup.
Indeed, goodness and steadfast love shall pursue me all the days of my life;
And I shall dwell in the house of Adonai as long as I live.

Kavanah

This is a time of pain. There is nothing you or anyone else can do to take away that pain or diminish it. Instead, you might look for people and spaces in your life that are able to contain your pain and to hold you.

Who are those people for you? What are those spaces for you? What might such a container look like for you?

Sacred Sources

> Do not console a person while the deceased is laying in front of them. (*Pirkei Avot* 4:18)

- The wisdom of *Pirkei Avot* teaches that when we are in our greatest pain, shocked, and overwhelmed by our loss, we cannot be comforted. Can you listen to the attempts of consolation from friends and family with a forgiving heart and ear?
- It is possible that the teaching from *Pirkei Avot* might also signal to us that the immediate time after experiencing a loss is not a time in which we are supposed to find comfort in the words of others—instead, we are supposed to do something else. What do you think your most important emotional tasks are at this time?
- Jewish tradition gives us a name for a person who has just experienced a significant loss and is preoccupied with organizing a funeral: *onein/on'nah* ("the person is in *aninut*," the period during which a mourner is preoccupied with the organizational aspects of losing a beloved person and has no time yet for the task of mourning). In what areas of your life do you still feel like an *onein/on'nah*, preoccupied by organizational and social tasks, unable to process, overwhelmed by pain, unreachable for consolation?

Poetry and Prayer

The Valley

Rabbi Karyn D. Kedar

The valley of the shadow of death is a tender place.
It is a place of questions and things unsaid.
And grace.
And love.
And depth.
And sadness.
My heart is open.
My breath is gentle.
I am tired and sleepless.
So I sit a while by the still waters
and You are with me.
God is with me.
I shall not fear.

Kaddish and Mourning Prayers

See page 175.

Week 5

Song

Oseh Shalom
Text: *Amidah*
Music: Robert Weinberg

עֹשֶׂה שָׁלוֹם בִּמְרוֹמָיו, הוּא יַעֲשֶׂה שָׁלוֹם עָלֵינוּ
וְעַל כָּל יִשְׂרָאֵל, וְאִמְרוּ: אָמֵן.

Oseh shalom bimromav, hu yaaseh shalom aleinu
v'al kol Yisrael, v'imru: Amen.

May the One who brings peace in the heavens, bring peace for us and for all Israel [and for all humankind], and let us say: *Amen*.

Kavanah

Sometimes, our lost loved ones seem to be close. We can see them in front of us; we reach to our phones to give them a call; we can hear their voices responding to our inner monologues. At other times, we suddenly get a sense of the emptiness their deaths leave behind.

When you stumble into a moment of emptiness, try not to rush through it. Whisper your goodbyes. Send your wishes for peace. Hold the face, the voice, and the presence of your loved one against your eyes, ears, and heart. Watch; listen; sense.

Sacred Sources

Rabbi Abba ben Rabbi Pappai and Rabbi Y'hoshua of Siknin said in the name of Rabbi Levi: For three days after death the soul hovers over the body, intending to reenter it; but as soon as it sees its appearance change, it departs. (*Vayikra Rabbah* 18:1)

- Does the image of the lingering soul make sense to you? Rationally? Emotionally?
- What do you think is the sensation Rabbi Levi tries to capture with the image of the lingering soul?
- What kinds of moments of farewell might you have experienced from your loved one?

Poetry and Prayer

To the God, Who Teaches

Rabbi Karyn D. Kedar

Do not fear the moment
when the border is near like the blue line,
thin upon the horizon.

Do not fear.

Dying is not a fearful thing.
Release the dread
like a child releases a helium balloon,
red, rising, toward the heavens,
the boundary between known and not known.

You cannot control this moment.
Not any of it.
Let go of the fear.

Rather, climb upon the seesaw,
and pray that the rocking
back and forth, back and forth,
be gentle, be kind.
One side, the weight of sadness,
the other the lift of love.
Love, sadness, love, sadness, sadness, love.
Back and forth, a gentle rocking
like it was, back in the womb.

And then,
the world contracts, becomes small.
Fewer visits, less talking, the bed envelops
the body that seems to disappear, sinking back
into the womb of preexistence.
Just breath, barely breath.
Swaying, sadness, love, sadness, love.
And the blue line nears,
the boundary emerges, envelops.
And all is peace.

No fear, only love.
Only love, a canopy of peace.

And then,
no longer a border, no longer the boundary,
but a hue between
now and eternity.

God, guard my parting and my return,
now and forever.
Amen. *Selah.*

Kaddish and Mourning Prayers

See page 175.

Week 6

Song

Bishvili Nivra HaOlam
Text: Babylonian Talmud, *Sanhedrin* 37a; Genesis 18:27
Music: Julie Geller

בִּשְׁבִילִי נִבְרָא הָעוֹלָם
וְאָנֹכִי עָפָר וָאֵפֶר.
Bishvili nivra haolam,
v'anochi afar va-eifer.

The world was created for me [Babylonian Talmud, *Sanhedrin* 37a],
I am dust and ashes [Genesis 18:27].

Kavanah

You might find yourself overwhelmed with organizational and social tasks. At times of change, much needs to be done. And yet, this is a time of loss, separation, and life-altering changes.

Take a moment to ask yourself: Where is your soul today? *What does it tell you? What is it busy with? What is happening in the most intimate chambers of your heart?*

Sacred Sources

The voices of five objects of creation go from one end of the world to the other, and their voices are inaudible. When people cut down the wood of the tree which yields fruit, its cry goes from one end of the world to the other, and the voice is inaudible. When the serpent sloughs off its skin, its cry goes from one end of the world to the other, and its voice is not heard. When a woman is divorced from her husband, her voice goes forth from one end of the world to the other, but the voice is inaudible. When the infant comes forth from its mother's womb. When the soul departs from the body, the cry goes forth from one end of the world to the other, and the voice is not heard. (*Pirkei D'Rabbi Eliezer* 34)

- What do the moments listed in *Pirkei D'Rabbi Eliezer* have in common? Do they all seem to belong in the same category? Which ones on this list surprise you?
- The sentences from *Pirkei D'Rabbi Eliezer* speak about pain. The moments of loss and inner breakings often come and go in silence; nothing in our appearance or in the appearance of the world reflects the painful emotions we contain in our bodies. In what ways does your pain express itself?
- Do you find comfort in the notion that our separation pains are noted by God? How do you think God looks at you at this time in your life?

Poetry and Prayer

From *Songs of Zion the Beautiful: 34*

Yehuda Amichai, translated by Chana Bloch

Let the memorial hill remember instead of me,
that's what it's here for. Let the park in-memory-of remember,
let the street that's-named-for remember,
let the well-known building remember,
let the synagogue that's named after God remember
let the rolling Torah scroll remember, let the prayer
for the memory of the dead remember. Let the flags remember
those multicolored shrouds of history: the bodies they wrapped
have long since turned to dust. Let the dust remember.
Let the dung remember at the gate. Let the afterbirth remember.
Let the beasts of the field and birds of the heavens
eat and remember.
Let all of them remember so that I can rest.

Kaddish and Mourning Prayers

See page 175.

Week 7

Song

Ham'chadeish
Text: Blessings before the *Sh'ma*
Music: Hazzan Joanna S. Dulkin

הַמְחַדֵּשׁ בְּכָל יוֹם תָּמִיד מַעֲשֵׂה בְרֵאשִׁית . . .
Ham'chadeish b'chol yom maaseih v'reishit . . .
Who renews every day the acts of creation . . .

Kavanah

We do not want to say goodbye. We do not want to accept. Our souls and hearts are ripped open by pain; our thoughts go in circles; our bodies are aching. We are not ready.

And yet, this experience of incompletion is a natural part of life. Few if any of us ever get to accomplish everything we hope to do in our lives. That can be a source of a great pain, and perhaps it might also inspire us to keep striving to meet our own goals and aspirations.

The loved one you lost also might not have been ready to leave. What would the person you lost have loved to do?

Sacred Sources

> Rav Chisda said, "A person's soul mourns for them during all seven days of mourning following their death, as it is stated, 'And his soul mourns in him' [Job 14:22], and it is also written, 'He observed a mourning ceremony of seven days for his father' [Genesis 50:10]." (Babylonian Talmud, *Shabbat* 152a)

- It might sometimes be hard for us when others/the community put a limit to the days or depth of our mourning. Without a doubt, there will be a part of our mourning when we will be alone. What are the possible advantages of a clearly defined mourning period?
- It is endlessly painful to let go. It might be unfathomable at

this time. How do you hold on to your loved one? How can you keep them present?

- What might it mean that a soul "is mourning *in* someone"? Does your mourning fill you out completely? When might that be true for you, and when might it not be true?

Poetry and Prayer

Loss-Change
Rabbi Eric Weiss

I don't need spices anymore
The salt drips from my eyes
The apples can keep their core
Mine is already hollowed.

I don't need to refrigerate anymore
Our bed is cold enough
The butter is safe
My heart is already churned.

I don't need the grocer anymore
My stomach has no craving
The earth can keep its bounty
You took mine.

With all we did, why did we never see a desert?
At least you might have taught me to live parched.

Kaddish and Mourning Prayers

See page 175.

BROKENNESS

You Were Taken from Me Too Early

Week 1

Song

Ratzo VaShov (Ebb and Flow)
Text: Based on Ezekiel 1:14
English Lyrics and Music: Cantor Lisa B. Segal

רָצוֹא וָשׁוֹב
Ratzo vashov, ebb and flow. (4x)

Here I am again, for the very first time—*Ratzo vashov*, ebb and flow,
Here I am, here I am, again and again—*Ratzo vashov*, ebb and flow,
Where have I been? Where am I going to?
Counting the days to the ebb and flow . . .

Kavanah

When we cry, the brain does not find peace—instead, crying allows emotions to rise with renewed intensity.

When you cry, let your tears, memories, and sadness flow. What images come up? What memories suddenly arise?

Sacred Sources

Rabbi Eliezer says: The night consists of three watches, and over each and every watch, the Holy One, blessed be God, sits and roars like a lion in pain over the destruction of the Temple. This imagery is derived from a reference in the Bible, as it is stated: "The Eternal 'roars' [*yishag*] from on high, God makes God's voice heard from the holy dwelling; God 'roars aloud' [*shaog yishag*] over the earthly abode; God utters shout like the grape traders, against all the dwellers on earth" (Jeremiah 25:30). The three instances of the root *shin-alef-gimel* in this verse correspond to the three watches of the night. (Babylonian Talmud, *B'rachot* 3a)

- The Talmud teaches that God is in pain, too—that God is weeping, moaning, and roaring in pain. How can we find comfort in the image of a God who is capable of the same kind of pain that each of us feels?

- In what ways can the image of a roaring God give us permission to roar with God, mourn with God, sit in our pain with God? In what ways might this image be unsettling to us?
- According to Rabbi Eliezer's teaching, God is overwhelmed by pain three times each night. God's pain has a rhythm just like ours. Pain and mourning become part of our daily and nightly lives. How do you learn to live with your pain? When does it come? When does it stay away? Do you already know when to expect it?

Poetry and Prayer

Lost and Found
Joy Ladin

You find yourself quite comfortable
in the bony clothes of death,
though you seem to have lost the feeling of,

well, feeling. Light moves through you
easily and eerily, as though life were a window
that was broken when you found it

so you can admire without shame
its fracture-stars
that never set, though you find you get a little lost

when you try to navigate by them
though the complicated waste
of loss and obligation

to the life that reveals itself
when you close your eyes,
the stars, that is, of the foundling self,

aroused and assertive, warmed by the hope
you found you've lost
in the bony clothes of death.

Kaddish and Mourning Prayers

See page 175.

Week 2

Song

Esa Chanfei Shachar
Text: Psalm 139:9–10
English Lyrics and Music: Cantor Abby Bernstein Gostein

Esa chanfei shachar	אֶשָּׂא כַנְפֵי שָׁחַר
eshk'nah b'acharit yam.	אֶשְׁכְּנָה בְּאַחֲרִית יָם.
Gam sham yadcha tancheini	גַּם שָׁם יָדְךָ תַנְחֵנִי
v'tochazeini y'minecha.	וְתֹאחֲזֵנִי יְמִינֶךָ.

If I take up the wings of the morning
And dwell on a distant shore
There Your hand will lead me
Your right hand will hold me forever.

Kavanah

Learning to live with a huge loss, we often are confronted with a deep sense of emptiness and disorientation. All we can see is what is no more. Our universe is empty and void.

When you are about to feel lost in sadness, emptiness, and despair, make sure that you are safe, warm, and well-fed. "Be your own best friend," as they say. Let comfort come. Take a moment to think: When and where do you stumble the most? When and where do you find rest to let your soul, heart, and mind catch up?

Sacred Sources

And the dust returns to the ground
As it was,
And the lifebreath returns to God
Who bestowed it.
Utter futility—said Koheleth—
All is futile!
(Ecclesiastes 12:7)

- The biblical Book of Ecclesiastes is a radical confrontation with the temporality of our lives. Everything that is alive, absolutely everything, dies at some point. Do you at times identify with Kohelet's sense that the fact of our temporality renders our lives meaningless?
- At other times, it might seem that it is exactly our lives' temporality that gives our days meaning. What are moments in which you have held both a sense of temporality and deep gratitude for being alive?
- This is a time when you might need to rethink the meaning of life itself, and your life specifically. How can you do that in a tender, loving way?

Poetry and Prayer

Revival
Luci Shaw

March. I am beginning
to anticipate a thaw. Early mornings
the earth, old unbeliever, is still crusted with frost
where the moles have nosed up their
cold castings, and the ground cover
in shadow under the cedars hasn't softened
for months, fogs layering their slow, complicated ice
around foliage and stem
night by night,

but as the light lengthens, preacher
of good news, evangelizing leaves and branches,
his large gestures beckon green
out of gray. Pinpricks of coral bursting
from the cotoneasters. A single bee
finding the white heather. Eager lemon-yellow
aconites glowing, low to the ground like
little uplifted faces. A crocus shooting up
a purple hand here, there, as I stand
on my doorstep, my own face drinking in heat

and light like a bud welcoming resurrection,
and my hand up, too, ready to sign on
for conversion.

Kaddish and Mourning Prayers

See page 175.

Week 3

Song

Ratzo VaShov (Ebb and Flow)
Text: Based on Ezekiel 1:14
English Lyrics and Music: Cantor Lisa B. Segal

רָצוֹא וָשׁוֹב.
Ratzo vashov, ebb and flow. (4x)

Here I am again, for the very first time—*Ratzo vashov*, ebb and flow,
Here I am, here I am, again and again—*Ratzo vashov*, ebb and flow,
Where have I been? Where am I going to?
Counting the days to the ebb and flow . . .

Kavanah

Pain and joy often come in waves. As we move through life, we are visited by both.

What is the rhythm of your pain? What is the rhythm of your joy?

Sacred Sources

For the same fate is in store for all: for the righteous, and for the wicked; for the good and pure, and for the impure; for those who sacrifice, and for those who do not; for those who are pleasing, and for those who are displeasing; and for those who swear, and for those who shun oaths. That is the sad thing about all that goes on under the sun: that the same fate is in store for all. (Not only that, but people's hearts are full of sadness, and their minds of madness, while they live; and then—to the dead!) . . .

I have further observed under the sun that
The race is not won by the swift,
Nor the battle by the valiant;
Nor is bread won by the wise,
Nor wealth by the intelligent,
Nor favor by the learned.

For the time of mischance comes to all. And one cannot even know one's time. As fish are enmeshed in a fatal net, and as birds are trapped in a snare, so we are caught at the time of calamity, when it comes upon us without warning. (Ecclesiastes 9:2–3, 9:11–12)

- The Book of Ecclesiastes makes us confront the fact that all of us need to live through pain, loss, injustice, and simply bad luck. And yet, its beautiful, poetic language suggests that its author(s) invested time and energy into the creation of something elegant and orderly in the midst of the painful chaos of our world, even if just for us, the readers. Where in your life do you create beauty and order for others?
- We might look at life as a series of lessons—lessons that challenge us to grow, to be who we are supposed to be, and to act as we are supposed to act, even in the midst of chaos, pain, and injustice. When do you feel overwhelmed by life's tasks? When do you feel that you mastered one?

Poetry and Prayer

Under the Harvest Moon
Carl Sandburg

Under the harvest moon,
When the soft silver
Drips shimmering
Over the garden nights,
Death, the gray mocker,
Comes and whispers to you
As a beautiful friend
Who remembers.

Under the summer roses
When the flagrant crimson
Lurks in the dusk
Of the wild red leaves,
Love, with little hands,
Comes and touches you

With a thousand memories,
And asks you
Beautiful, unanswerable questions.

Kaddish and Mourning Prayers

See page 175.

Week 4

Song

Lamdeini
Text: Leah Goldberg
Music: Cantor Benjie Ellen Schiller

לַמְּדֵנִי אֱלֹהַי, בָּרֵךְ וְהִתְפַּלֵּל,
לַמֵּד אֶת שִׂפְתוֹתַי בְּרָכָה וְשִׁיר הַלֵּל.

Lamdeini Elohai, bareich v'hitpaleil,
Lameid et siftotai b'rachah v'shir hallel.

Teach me, O God, a blessing, a prayer
on the mystery of a withered leaf,
on ripened fruit so fair,
on the freedom to see,
to sense, to breathe,
to know, to hope,
to despair.

Kavanah

You might be experiencing a kind of pain you have never felt before. It may feel like you have lost your will to plow through the heavy mud of pain, heaviness, loneliness, and despair. It is too painful; it is too difficult; it takes too long.

Take a break. Watch a movie. Listen to a song. Go for a walk. Read. Take your mind off its tasks. Sometimes, it is okay to put a task to the side for a while. Let go. Maybe there, in that place of rest, new energy and understanding wait for you.

Sacred Sources

"Illness is the night-side of life, a more onerous citizenship. Everyone who is born holds dual citizenship, in the kingdom of the well and the kingdom of the sick. Although we all prefer to use only the good passport, sooner or later each of us is obliged, at least for a spell, to identify ourselves as citizens of that other place." . . . Susan Sontag argues convincingly against this message of assigning meaning to pain. It "assigns to the luckless ill the ultimate responsibility both for falling ill and for getting well." That is to say: It causes damage. (Lawrence A. Hoffman, *The Journey Home: Discovering the Spiritual Wisdom of the Jewish Tradition*, pp. 160 [quoting Susan Sontag], 171)

- Reading Susan Sontag and reflecting on the fact that all of us know of sickness, pain, and death, Lawrence Hoffman warns us not to look for responsibility. No one deserves to become sick, to live with pain, to die. Yet, we all must come to terms with this reality. What might make it possible for to you to accept this fact?
- What are the advantages of our attempts to ignore this night-side of life? What does this ignorance make possible?
- How can we speak about the night-side of life with empathy for ourselves and for those who live in it? How can we create respect and dignity for those who need to travel to this "other place"?

Poetry and Prayer

Hope

Reverend Victoria Safford

Our mission is to plant ourselves at the gates of hope.
Not the prudent gates of optimism which are somewhat narrower,
Nor the stalwart, boring gates of common sense,
Nor the strident gates of self-righteousness which creak on shrill and angry hinges,
Nor the cheerful, flimsy garden gate of everything is gonna be all right.
But a very different, sometimes very lonely place.
The place of truth telling
about your own soul first of all and its condition
the place of resistance and defiance.
The piece of ground from which you see the world both as

it is and as it could be
As it might be, as it will be.
The place from which you glimpse not only struggle
But joy in the struggle.
And we stand there
All of us
Beckoning and calling,
Telling people what we are seeing
Asking people what they see.

Kaddish and Mourning Prayers

See page 175.

Week 5

Song

Esa Chanfei Shachar
Text: Psalm 139:9–10
English Lyrics and Music: Cantor Abby Bernstein Gostein

אֶשָּׂא כַנְפֵי שָׁחַר אֶשְׁכְּנָה בְּאַחֲרִית יָם.
גַּם שָׁם יָדְךָ תַנְחֵנִי וְתֹאחֲזֵנִי יְמִינֶךָ.

Esah chanfei shachar eshk'nah b'acharit yam.
Gam sham yadcha tancheini v'tochazeini y'minecha.

If I take up the wings of the morning
And dwell on a distant shore
There Your hand will lead me
Your right hand will hold me forever.

Kavanah

Sometimes our emotions are simply out of control. Each day, each hour, we go back and forth between calm and chaos, anger and comforting memories, a renewed sense of being alive and complete brokenness. The hardest part of all might be that we don't know when this roller coaster of emotions will end.

Mindfulness teachings ask us to take a step back. Watch your emotions come and go; rise and dissolve, like a stream of air. You are sitting in the midst of this stream. Just watch. Do not try to stop the flow.

Sacred Sources

For the leader. On *ayelet ha-shachar*. A Psalm of David.

My God, my God,
why have You abandoned me;
why are You so far from delivering me
and from my anguished roaring?
My God,
I cry by day—You answer not;

by night, and have no respite. . . .
You drew me from the womb,
made me secure at my mother's breast.
I became Your charge at birth;
from my mother's womb You have been my God.
Do not be far from me,
for trouble is near,
and there is none to help.
(Psalm 22:1–3, 10–12)

- Psalm 22 is a good example of the mix of emotions a person in mourning is familiar with: at times, we feel abandoned; at others, we feel held by the care of others and God. Which other emotions do you discern in the words of the Psalmist?
- Which of these biblical metaphors speak to you? If they do not speak to you, what metaphors would you prefer?
- The Psalmist asks "why" three times at the start of this short psalm. What response would you offer? How might trusting in God's *chesed*/kindness offer some glimmer of hope even in the midst of this great uncertainty?

Poetry and Prayer

A Psalm of Found Joy: For the First Joy in Months
Devon A. Spier

I found my joy.
She wasn't hiding.
She was waiting.
For the moment to lean forward,
To come from the middle of my chest,
Open up my throat.
And laugh without holding back.

"Adonai will do great things for us and we shall rejoice" (Psalm 126:3).

Kaddish and Mourning Prayers

See page 175.

Week 6

Song

Lamdeini
Text: Leah Goldberg
Music: Cantor Benjie Ellen Schiller

לַמְּדֵנִי אֱלֹהַי, בָּרֵךְ וְהִתְפַּלֵּל,
לַמֵּד אֶת שְׂפָתוֹתַי בְּרָכָה וְשִׁיר הַלֵּל.

Lamdeini Elohai, bareich v'hitpaleil,
Lameid et siftotai b'rachah v'shir hallel.

Teach me, O God, a blessing, a prayer
on the mystery of a withered leaf,
on ripened fruit so fair,
on the freedom to see,
to sense, to breathe,
to know, to hope,
to despair.

Kavanah

Our mourning does not always take the shape we have been expecting. Sometimes we are shocked by the intensity of anger, fear, and aggression we experience—anger at God or the person we lost; anger at doctors or well-meaning friends and family members; anger at ourselves. Fear from the changed life ahead of us. Fear of a different financial situation. Aggression toward colleagues and bosses who might demand us to function at times when we cannot.

Give yourself spaces to scream—even if it is into the pillows. Give yourself time to vent, to break down, to stop. Find body movements to release some of the tension you might carry in your body.

Sacred Sources

A Song, a song of the sons of Korach, For the conductor: on *Machalat L'anot*, a *maskil* of Heiman the Ezrachite.

Adonai, God of my deliverance,
I have cried out by day and in the night before You:
Let my prayer precede me in Your presence,
Incline Your ear to my ringing cry!

For my being is mired in miseries,
And my life draws near to Sheol.
I am reckoned with those who go down to the Pit;
I am like one abandoned by those who assist,
Cut loose among the dead,
Like the slain splayed out in the grave
To whom no one pays heed any longer,
Who are cut off from Your hand.
You have bundled me away in the bottommost pit,
In dark places, in the depths.
Your wrath weighs me down,
With all Your crashing waves You afflicted me—selah!

You distanced my intimates from me,
You made me like pagan idols for them,
I am bound in jail and cannot break free.
My eye grows weak from isolation,
I have called upon you, Adonai, every day,
I have spread out my hands to You—

Will You do wonders for the dead?
Will shades arise, giving thanks to You?—selah!
Will stories of Your covenantal love be spun inside the grave,
Of Your faithful oversight in Oblivion?
Will Your wonders be known in the darkness,
And Your justice in the land of forgetfulness?
But I, alive, cry to You, Adonai,
And in the morning my prayer comes to greet You—
Why, Adonai, do You spurn my whole being,
Hiding Your face from me?
Sigh do I, perishing since puberty;
I have borne Your blows, I am benumbed!
Your wrath has passed over me,
Your terrors have terminated me!
They surrounded me like water all day long,
They hemmed me in together.
You have distanced lover and companion from me—
My intimates are darkness.
(Psalm 88)

- Psalm 88 is one of the darkest among our collection of 150 psalms. The Bible makes space for despair and anger—and a deep sense of loneliness. Sometimes it is helpful to know that we are not the first who felt those emotions rising in us. When are you or have you been experiencing these kinds of emotions?
- The text of Psalm 88 also expresses anger at God. "Why have You left me? Why do you attack me?" asks the Psalmist. Do you find yourself accusing God? Of what? How does your anger sound?
- Mourning is not always quiet; mourning does not always need to sound nice. Which of the verses of Psalm 88 speak to you, personally? And if you do not find any that do, can you write your own?

Poetry and Prayer

For Weeks after the Funeral
Andrea Hollander Budy

The house felt like the opera,
the audience in their seats, hushed, ready,
but the cast not yet arrived.

And if I said anything
to try to appease the anxious air, my words
would hang alone like the single chandelier

waiting to dim the auditorium, but still
too huge, too prominent, too bright, its light
announcing only itself, bringing more

emptiness into the emptiness.

Kaddish and Mourning Prayers

See page 175.

Week 7

Song

Eil Na R'fa Na Lah
Text: Based on Numbers 12:13 and the Serenity Prayer
Music: Rabbi Or Zohar

אֵל נָא רְפָא נָא לָהּ.

אֱלֹהִים תֵּן בִּי שַׁלְוָה,
לְקַבֵּל אֶת מָה שֶׁלֹּא בִּיתָן לְשַׁנּוֹת.
וֶאֱלֹהִים תֵּן בִּי הָאֹמֶץ,
לְשַׁנּוֹת אֶת מָה שֶׁבִּיתָן לְשַׁנּוֹת.
וְתֵן בִּי אֶת הַחָכְמָה,
לְהַבְחִין בֵּין זֶה לָזֶה.

מִי שֶׁבֵּרַךְ אֲבוֹתֵינוּ,
הוּא יְרַפֵּא אֶת הַחוֹלִים,
מְקוֹר שְׁכִינָה לְאִמּוֹתֵינוּ,
הִיא תִּמְצָא מָזוֹר לַסּוֹבְלִים,
רְפוּאַת הַנֶּפֶשׁ וְהַגּוּף,
רְפוּאָה שְׁלֵמָה.

God, please heal her.

God, grant me the serenity
to accept the things I cannot change.
God, grant me the courage
to change the things I can.
And God, grant me the wisdom
to know the difference.

May God who has blessed the generations
bless and heal all who are ill.
May the love and mercy of *Shechinah*
ease the pain of all those in need,
healing the body and the soul.
Whole healing.

Kavanah

When mourning, we have to learn to raise our voices. We have to learn to speak about our pain, to bring forth our accusations, doubts, needs, and pleas. Sometimes, it is hard to find people who will listen to us, especially if we feel the need to revisit similar thoughts over and over again.

Take a moment and think about the weeks and maybe months of your mourning up until this point. Which thoughts and emotions have become steady companions? Which ones have visited less frequently? Which ones may have disappeared over the course of the last weeks?

Sacred Sources

I have called on Your name, O Eternal,
From the depths of the Pit.
Hear my plea;
Do not shut Your ear
To my groan, to my cry!
You have ever drawn nigh when I called You;
You have said, "Do not fear!"
You championed my cause, O Eternal,
You have redeemed my life.
(Lamentations 3:55–58)

- The Book of Lamentations speaks about the "pit" in which we find ourselves when mourning. What would you take with you into your pit? Which objects carry your memories and give you comfort?
- Remember a moment in which someone told you "not to fear." What do you fear? Is there someone whose comfort could help you through that fear?
- Take stock of the things surrounding you. Which ones remind you of the person you lost? Do you feel close enough to those objects?

Poetry and Prayer

Everything That Was Broken
Mary Oliver

Everything that was broken has
forgotten its brokenness. I live
now in a sky-house, through every
window the sun. Also, your presence.
Our touching, our stories. Earthy
and holy both. How can this be, but
it is. Every day has something in
it whose name is Forever.

Kaddish and Mourning Prayers

See page 175.

SADNESS

How Can I Live without You?

Week 1

Song

Healer of the Broken-Hearted
Text: Psalm 147:3–4
Music: Shir Yaakov Feit

Harofei lishvurei lev	הָרֹפֵא לִשְׁבוּרֵי לֵב
Um'chabeish l'atzvotam	וּמְחַבֵּשׁ לְעַצְּבוֹתָם
Moneh mispar lakochavim	מוֹנֶה מִסְפָּר לַכּוֹכָבִים
L'chulam sheimot yikra . . .	לְכֻלָּם שֵׁמוֹת יִקְרָא . . .

Healer of the broken-hearted
Binder of our wounds
Counter of uncountable stars
You know who we are . . .

Kavanah

Sadness often has a very specific weight. We can feel that weight on our chest, on our shoulders, in our chest, beyond our eyelids.

How much does your sadness weigh? What color does it have? How would you describe it to someone else?

Sacred Sources

Sarah lived to be 127 years old—such was the span of Sarah's life. . . . And Abraham proceeded to mourn for Sarah and to bewail her. (Genesis 23:1–2)

To mourn . . . and to bewail her. Usually weeping precedes eulogizing because the mourner's sense of loss diminishes with time. In Sarah's case, however, her absence was felt more each day. (Kli Yakar on Genesis 23:2)

- We often hear that time heals all wounds. This is not always true. Some wounds, we know, stay open—though, hopefully, we learn to live with them. Thinking about your own mourning, at which times have you wanted to cry? At which times have you wanted to talk?

- Jewish mourning traditions set us different times to assess our pain and to share our memories: the seven days of shivah, the thirty days of *sh'loshim*, the months leading up to *matzeivah* (unveiling of the tombstone), and the end of the first year of mourning—and then, of course, the yearly *yahrzeit* of our beloved's death. Those dates are helpful, but they do not necessarily overlap entirely with our personal mourning experience. What dates and periods have turned into meaningful markers for you? Which ones do you anticipate doing so?
- How old was the person you are mourning? What is the significance of that number to you?
- When we mourn over someone, we stay close to them emotionally. When or where do you feel closest to the person for whom you are mourning?

Poetry and Prayer

Five Stages of Grief
Linda Pastan

The night I lost you
someone pointed me towards
the Five Stages of Grief
Go that way, they said,
    it's easy, like learning to climb
stairs after the amputation.
And so I climbed.
    Denial was first.
I sat down at breakfast
    carefully setting the table
    for two. I passed you the toast—
you sat there. I passed
you the paper—you hid
behind it.
Anger seemed more familiar.
I burned the toast, snatched
the paper and read the headlines myself.
But they mentioned your departure,

and so I moved on to
Bargaining. What could I exchange
for you? The silence
after storms? My typing fingers?
Before I could decide, *Depression*
came puffing up, a poor relation
its suitcase tied together
with string. In the suitcase
were bandages for the eyes
and bottles of sleep. I slid
all the way down the stairs
feeling nothing.
And all the time Hope
flashed on and off
in defective neon.
Hope was a signpost pointing
straight in the air.
Hope was my uncle's middle name,
he died of it.
After a year I am still climbing, though my feet slip
on your stone face.
The treeline
has long since disappeared;
green is a color
I have forgotten.
But now I see what I am climbing
towards: *Acceptance*
written in capital letters,
a special headline:
Acceptance
its name is in lights.
I struggle on,
waving and shouting.
Below, my whole life spreads its surf,
all the landscapes I've ever known
or dreamed of. Below
a fish jumps: the pulse

in your neck.
Acceptance. I finally
        reach it.
But something is wrong.
Grief is a circular staircase.
I have lost you.

Kaddish and Mourning Prayers

See page 175.

Week 2

Song

Achat Sha'alti
Text: adapted from Psalm 27:4
Music: Chava Mirel

Achat shaalti otah avakeish	אַחַת שָׁאַלְתִּי אוֹתָהּ אֲבַקֵּשׁ
Shivti, shivti b'veit Adonai	שִׁבְתִּי, שִׁבְתִּי בְּבֵית יְיָ
Shivti, shivti kol y'mei chayai	שִׁבְתִּי, שִׁבְתִּי כָּל־יְמֵי חַיַּי
Lachazot b'noam Adonai	לַחֲזוֹת בְּנֹעַם יְיָ
Ul'vakeir b'heichalo	וּלְבַקֵּר בְּהֵיכָלוֹ
Lachazot b'noam Adonai	לַחֲזוֹת בְּנֹעַם יְיָ

To gaze upon the beauty of Adonai
One thing, one thing I ask You, Adonai:
To be with You all of my life.

Kavanah

No one can be replaced—no life is equal to another. That emptiness may linger for a long time.

Share a story about the person you are mourning with someone. How does sharing a memory fill a bit of that emptiness?

Sacred Sources

The midrash suggests that the biblical patriarch Isaac suffered greatly after the death of his mother and that he mourned her for a long time. The passage below is an interpretation of what happened after Rebekah became Isaac's wife. It describes how four sources of support and comfort for Isaac disappeared after his mother's death, and how they were restored after Rebekah came into his life.

> *Isaac then brought her [Rebekah] into the tent of his mother Sarah* (Genesis 24:67): All the days that Sarah was alive, a cloud was connected to the entrance of her tent. When she died, the cloud stopped [resting at her tent]. And when Rebekah came, the cloud returned. All the days that Sarah was alive, the doors were open wide. When she

died, the wideness stopped. And when Rebekah came, the wideness returned. And all the days that Sarah was alive, there was a blessing in her dough, and when Sarah died, that blessing ended. When Rebekah came, the blessing returned. All the days that Sarah was alive, there was a candle that would burn from Sabbath Eve to the next Sabbath Eve, and when she died, the candle stopped [burning for so long]. And when Rebekah came, [the weeklong flame] returned. (*B'reishit Rabbah* 60:16)

Each of these four constants symbolizes a different aspect of Isaac's life, dimmed through the pain of losing his mother. For him, his mother was a connection to God. Her religious spirit brought God close, and when she passed away, Isaac felt himself not only far from her, but also from his creator. He did not know how to access God without her near. Sarah was also a connection to hospitality and openness. . . . When she died, Isaac saw that the world was a little less just. Then there was the loss of her piety. Dough and lamps are meant to symbolize ritual connections. Sarah observed the rituals of Shabbat as no other did and no other could. For Isaac, the Sabbath would be less rich and beautiful without her in it. (Marc Katz, *The Heart of Loneliness: How Jewish Wisdom Can Help You Cope and Find Comfort*, p. 53)

- What are the "constants" that you feel are missing the most from your life during this time of mourning?
- What, if anything, is helping you to meet the emptiness?
- What role might other family members or friends play in helping you to dim your fear and/or reverence of the emptiness? What would you ask for if you could?

Poetry and Prayer

Just Delicate Needles

Rolf Jacobsen

It's so delicate, the light.
And there's so little of it. The dark
is huge.
Just delicate needles, the light,
in an endless night.

And it has such a long way to go
through such desolate space

So let's be gentle with it.
Cherish it.
So it will come again in the morning.
We hope.

Kaddish and Mourning Prayers

See page 175.

Week 3

Song

Min Hameitzar
Text: Psalm 118:5
Music: Rabbi Deborah Sacks Mintz

מִן הַמֵּצַר קָרָאתִי יָּהּ,
עָנָנִי בַמֶּרְחָב יָהּ.

Min hameitzar karati Yah,
anani vamerchav Yah.

From the straits I called out to *Yah*,
Yah answered me from a wide-open expanse.

Kavanah

Sometimes we find comfort in our memories, sometimes in the love of people surrounding us—sometimes in our friends or family; sometimes in strangers or books or movies that surprise us with the right words at exactly the right time.

From time to time, you might find that breathing comes easier to you. As you become familiar with a new reality with the steady presence of memory, you find yourself settling into a new sense of self. Heavy? Yes. Sad? Yes. But without any doubt, you.

Sacred Sources

More than any other part of scripture, we can say that the psalms are not beloved because they are holy, but that they are holy because they are beloved. . . . We read psalms because they help us confront the pains and challenges that are part of every human life. Psalms help us put into words what we experience and feel; more than that, many will tell you, psalms help us overcome our problems and bear the burdens that life places on all of us. (Daniel Polish, *Bringing the Psalms to Life*, pp. xii–xiii)

To the lead player. A Psalm of David.

How long, O Eternal, will You forget me always?
How long hide Your face from me?
How long shall I cast about for counsel,
  sorrow in my heart all day?
How long will my enemy loom over me?
Regard, answer me, O Eternal, my God.
Light up my eyes, lest I sleep death,
Lest my enemy say, "I've prevailed over them,"
Lest my foes exult when I stumble.
But I in Your kindness do trust,
My heart exults in Your rescue.
Let me sing to Adonai
For God requited me.
  (Psalm 13)

- Who are the "enemies" that keep you in the dark?
- Where are the glimpses of light?
- How might you understand God as a source of comfort, kindness, and healing?

Poetry and Prayer

Uncharted Territory
Hilda Yael Kessler

    Start anew
in uncharted territory
    seek
the unknown coastline
the unrecognized terrain
the language
    foreign to heart and soul.

    I tremble at my task
        I have not been endowed
            with great strength
            or powerful skills

my means are meager
my support in doubt.
Yet persevere I must
to continue my journey
bringing forth the word
proclaiming:
we are the children of prophets
are charged to start anew
fulfilling the purpose
given us.

To start anew in
grace
bringing forth
the word of words
guiding our path in
uncharted
territory.

Kaddish and Mourning Prayers

See page 175.

Week 4

Song

Ayekah? Hineini.
Text: Genesis 3:9 and 22:1
Music: Cantor Lisa B. Segal

אַיֶּכָּה? הִנֵּנִי.
Ayekah? Hineini.
Where are you? I am right here.

Kavanah

Sometimes our mourning does not allow us to find any language adequate for the emotions we are living through.

If you are journaling, leave one page blank. If you are sitting with a friend, ask to just sit there for a while without talking. If you are by yourself, take some time to just look out of the window. Let the silence be.

Sacred Sources

Now Aaron's sons Nadab and Abihu each took his fire pan, put fire in it, and laid incense on it; and they offered before the Eternal alien fire. . . . And fire came forth from the Eternal and consumed them. . . . And Aaron was silent. (Leviticus 10:1–3)

The Gemara explains: And what is different about lentils, that they in particular are the fare customarily offered to mourners? They say in the West, in *Eretz Yisrael*, in the name of Rabba bar Mari: Just as this lentil has no mouth, i.e., it does not have a crack like other legumes, so too a mourner has no mouth, that is, one's anguish prevents one from speaking. Alternatively, just as this lentil is completely round, so too mourning comes around to the inhabitants of the world. (Babylonian Talmud, *Bava Batra* 16b)

The Gemara returns to examining the *halachot* (laws) of consolation. Rabbi Yochanan said: The consolers are not permitted to speak words of consolation until the mourner opens and speaks first. As it is stated: "And they sat down with him upon the ground for seven days and seven nights, and none spoke a word to him; for they saw that his suffering was very great. After this Job opened his mouth" (Job 2:13–3:1). And afterward: "And Eliphaz the Temanite answered and said" (Job 4:1). (Babylonian Talmud, *Mo-eid Katan* 28b)

- In the biblical text, Aaron utters no words after the death of his two sons. Instead, he continues to do what needs to be done. Are you familiar with moments in which you preferred to act, instead of talk? How can silent activity be helpful?
- The Talmud takes the story of Job's friends sharing in his silence and turns it into part of our mourning customs. Think about the people—or animals—with whom you can share your silence. Who are they? What makes them special to you?

Poetry and Prayer

Don't Distance Yourself

Zelda, translated by Rabbi Steven Sager

The comforters who come to the courtyard
—the outer one—
stand near the gate
that faces the valley of the shadow of death
with its terror all around.
Standing near the gate is as much
As the comforters can bear.
Even my soul is miles away
From the crying I. It's a fact.

Fashioner of nights and spirit
surely against you rises this awful cry,
don't distance yourself—
don't let millions of light years
stand as a barrier
between you and Job.

Kaddish and Mourning Prayers

See page 175.

Week 5

Song

Min Hameitzar
Text: Psalm 118:5
Music: Rabbi Deborah Sacks Mintz

מִן הַמֵּצַר קָרָאתִי יָּהּ,
עָנָנִי בַמֶּרְחָב יָהּ.

Min hameitzar karati Yah,
anani vamerchav Yah.

From the straits I called out to *Yah*,
Yah answered me from a wide-open expanse.

Kavanah

In life, the boundaries between joy and mourning, past and future, peace and conflict, often become blurry. Instead of the orderly categories we are used to read about, we often need to navigate a wild mix of sad and happy, easy and difficult, beautiful and ugly.

Stretch the muscles of your heart. What were moments of joy in the midst of your stream of sadness? When was your new life of mourning disrupted by a surprising moment of ease and enjoyment or maybe even just comfort and a sense of safety?

Sacred Sources

In the case of one who buries their dead relative three days before a pilgrimage festival, the decree of the seven-day period of mourning is nullified for them. If one buries their dead relative eight days before a festival, the decree of thirty days is nullified for them, and therefore he may cut his hair on the eve of the festival. (Babylonian Talmud, *Mo-eid Katan* 19b)

The Sages taught: During the first three days after one's bereavement, a mourner is prohibited from working, even if one is a poor person who is supported by charity. From this point forward, one may do work privately in one's own home if one needs to do so. And similarly a woman may spin thread on a spindle in her own home when she is mourning. The Sages also taught: A mourner during the first three days after bereavement may not go to another mourner's. (Babylonian Talmud, *Mo-eid Katan* 21b)

- Jewish law describes days and periods of time during which the public display of mourning is forbidden. We are, even as mourners, sometimes asked to join in the joyous occasions of family, friends, or our communities. What are ways in which this is possible for you? When do you find yourself unable to share in the joys of others?
- The list of days and periods of times during which mourning is forbidden includes the pilgrimage festivals of Pesach, Shavuot, and Sukkot; the High Holy Days (Rosh HaShanah and Yom Kippur); and many family *simchas* and work obligations. What do you think of these limitations to your mourning? What are times and occasions that limit your own grief?
- We often will not be able to "postpone" our mourning and will spend time at festive meals, weddings, and other happy occasions while we still feel heavy, lonely, and sad. What are ways that seem helpful to you in navigating those tensions?

Poetry and Prayer

From *In My Life, On My Life*
Yehuda Amichai

And every person is a dam between the past and future.
When he dies, the dam is broken and the past bursts through
into the future,
And there is no early and no late, and time, is one time,
Like our God, our time is one.
And the memory of the dam is a blessing.

Kaddish and Mourning Prayers

See page 175.

Week 6

Song

Ayekah? Hineini.
Text: Genesis 3:9 and 22:1
Music: Cantor Lisa B. Segal

אַיֶּכָּה? הִנֵּנִי.
Ayekah? Hineini.
Where are you? I am right here.

Kavanah

When we mourn the loss of a beloved person, almost all of us begin to ask big questions: What is the value of relationships, when we know that they will all end one day? How do we want to live and shape the relationships we are in? How do we want to be remembered? What is the meaning we want to give to our own lives?

In moments in which you think about these big questions, who are you thinking about? Who are your role models? Who is your inspiration? How do you not *want to live?*

Sacred Sources

> Exalted and hallowed be God's great name in the world which God created, according to plan. May God's majesty be revealed in the days of our lifetime and the life of all Israel—speedily, imminently, to which we say Amen. . . . Blessed, praised, honored, exalted, extolled, glorified, adored, and lauded be the name of the Holy Blessed One, beyond all earthly words and songs of blessing, praise, and comfort. To which we say Amen. (*Kaddish*)

- Traditionally, we are asked to respond to the news of someone's death with *Baruch dayan ha-emet*—"Blessed is the true Judge." This traditional response affirms God's justice—at a moment when we might feel the opposite or, frankly, God's total absence. What is the meaning of praising and affirming

God in moments in which our hearts are broken? What do we provide to others and to ourselves by saying them?

- The words of the *Kaddish* are vibrant in their ancient, repetitive rhythm: "Blessed, praised, honored, exalted, extolled, glorified, adored, and lauded be the name." Write your own *Kaddish* line. What words of praise do you find for God?
- Some Jews believe that the poetry of the *Kaddish* helps the soul of our loved ones to rise to heaven. If you could give the soul you lost some words on its way, what would you say? Which words do you carry deep within you?

Poetry and Prayer

Grief in Haiku
Deborah Greene

The journey through grief
So vast, dark, and uncertain
Where is my compass

God, are You with me
I search, eyes closed, heart open
Oh Source of comfort

I cry out in tears
A primal ache in my soul
Help me to find You

Prayer is hard for me
How do I speak to You God
Tears flow down my cheeks

They carry in them
All the words I cannot say
Hear them God, hear them . . .

I ask, *Ayekah*?
In the still quiet moments
The wind whispers back

I listen closely
Hineni, the wind calls out
Here I am, with You

The journey is long
The gentle breeze carries me
Forward with God's grace

Kaddish and Mourning Prayers

See page 175.

Week 7

Song

Healer of the Broken-Hearted
Text: Psalm 147:3–4
Music: Shir Yaakov Feit

Harofei lishvurei lev — הָרֹפֵא לִשְׁבוּרֵי לֵב
Um'chabeish l'atzvotam — וּמְחַבֵּשׁ לְעַצְּבוֹתָם
Moneh mispar lakochavim — מוֹנֶה מִסְפָּר לַכּוֹכָבִים
L'chulam sheimot yikra . . . — לְכֻלָּם שֵׁמוֹת יִקְרָא . . .

Healer of the broken-hearted
Binder of our wounds
Counter of uncountable stars
You know who we are . . .

Kavanah

Sometimes during a period of mourning, we might suddenly realize—with guilt? shame? surprise? gratitude?—that we have not been thinking of our loss for a couple of minutes or hours. We were focused on work, a conversation with a friend, a movie, or another problem in our life.

Whenever this happens, do not be afraid. It does not mean that you are forgetting the person you loved. It means that life is bringing more to you than just this loss—and that life itself demands your attention.

Sacred Sources

God heals their broken hearts
and binds up their wounds.
(Psalm 147:3)

- Have you had a sense, in the last weeks, that your heart might slowly be healing? What feelings accompany this process?
- The verse from Psalm 147 seems to say that God wants our hearts to heal, that we are not supposed to spend the rest of

our lives in mourning. What do you think of God's wish? Is it one you can share at times? If not, why not?

- Think back to a time of healing in your life, physically or emotionally. How did you experience it at the time? What was necessary for your healing? What disturbed you in that process?

Poetry and Prayer

Dropping Stones from the Heart (with chest-pounding)
In memory of Rabbi Rachel Cowan
Rabbi Pamela Wax

Take your right hand
and pound your heart,
palm open,
for each of the six days
of Creation

Immediately drop your hand
to a resting place,
like Shabbat,
sinking to stillness

Repeat seven beats seven times
as time deepens into time,
hours into days
and days into weeks,
Omer periods, months,
shmitta years and *yovel* years,
millennia and eons and ages,
Ice Age and Bronze Age
Iron Age, New Age,
and Wise Age

Six times I pound then drop,
pound then drop the stones
I carry needlessly
heedlessly

On Yom Kippur we confess
and pound our chest
in remembrance of things past
where we have erred needlessly
heedlessly

Sometimes we rub gently to open
our hearts to the clarity
the hope
and the movement toward wisdom
and compassion

But remember.
Remember to drop the hand to stillness
to honor Shabbat
to honor the inside passage to
wisdom

Kaddish and Mourning Prayers

See page 175.

COMFORT

Seeking Support

Week 1

Song

Asher Yatzar
Text: Morning Blessings, *Birchot HaShachar*
English Lyrics and Music: Dan Nichols

I thank You for my life, body and soul.
Help me realize I'm beautiful and whole.
I'm perfect the way I am
And a little broken too.
I will live each day as a gift I give to you.

בָּרוּךְ אַתָּה, יְיָ, רוֹפֵא כָל בָּשָׂר וּמַפְלִיא לַעֲשׂוֹת.
Baruch atah, Adonai, rofei chol basar umafli laasot. (2x)
Blessed are You, Adonai, the wondrous healer of all flesh.

Kavanah

You buried a loved one. You had to let someone go. Think about the site you visited for their funeral. Think about the place you saw your beloved person for the last time; think about the places you visited together.

Hold up this inner map. It tells the story of your relationship.

Sacred Sources

The woman was left without her two sons and without her husband. She started out with her daughters-in-law to return from the country of Moab; for in the country of Moab she had heard that the Eternal had taken note of God's people and given them food. Accompanied by her two daughters-in-law, she left the place where she had been living; and they set out on the road back to the land of Judah. But Naomi said to her two daughters-in-law, "Turn back, each of you to her mother's house. May the Eternal deal kindly with you, as you have dealt with the dead and with me! . . ." And she kissed them farewell. They broke into weeping and said to her,

"No, we will return with you to your people." But Naomi replied, "Turn back, my daughters! . . ." They broke into weeping again, and Orpah kissed her mother-in-law farewell. But Ruth clung to her. . . . Ruth replied, "Do not urge me to leave you, to turn back and not follow you. For wherever you go, I will go; wherever you lodge, I will lodge; your people shall be my people, and your God my God. Where you die, I will die, and there I will be buried." (Ruth 1:5–17)

- The Book of Ruth tells a story about loyalty. Naomi's daughter-in-law Ruth does not abandon her mother-in-law when she is alone, without any means, and returning to a country that is completely foreign to Ruth. Ruth insists on remaining Naomi's companion. What does this kind of loyalty remind you of? Where can you find it in your own life?
- For all of us, friends, family, and colleagues who accompany us for many years hold a special place in our hearts. Think about some of those people in your own life. How would you characterize the companionship that each of them offers you?
- Naomi struggles with accepting the companionship Ruth offers to her. How familiar are you with this struggle? Do you welcome people into your life who offer their companionship to you?

Poetry and Prayer

Meditation on Mitzvot

Alden Solovy

It's simple, really,
This list of things we do,
As a people,
This list of things I do,
To live in a good way,
For others and myself,
To leave a legacy of love,
To leave the world
Just a little better each day.

A kind word.
A gentle hand.
A loving voice.
A giving heart.

It's not so simple, really,
To remember to live this way.
Always.
So we arrive early to study Torah
And strive for devotion in prayer,
To remember to honor all beings
With compassion and understanding,
Living a life of mitzvot in joy and service,
So that Torah will resound from our hearts,
Through our words and deeds,
Into the world,
And into the generations to come.

Kaddish and Mourning Prayers

See page 175.

Week 2

Song

Mozi's *Nigun* (*Ana B'cho-ach*)
Text: *Ana B'cho-ach—Kabbalat Shabbat* Liturgy
Music: Joey Weisenberg

אָנָּא בְּכֹחַ גְּדֻלַּת יְמִינְךָ. תַּתִּיר צְרוּרָה,
קַבֵּל רִנַּת עַמְּךָ. שַׂגְּבֵנוּ טַהֲרֵנוּ נוֹרָא.

Ana b'cho-ach g'dulat y'mincha. Tatir tz'rurah,
kabeil rinat amcha. Sagveinu tahareinu nora.

We beg You with the strength and greatness of Your right arm.
Untangle our knotted fate,
Accept Your people's song. Elevate and purify us, Awesome One.

Kavanah

It is often the small gestures of friends, family, and colleagues that give us the most comfort—but we can also comfort ourselves.

Today, nourish yourself with something you love: some food, a piece of music or music-making, a walk, a workout, flowers, art, arts and crafts, sleep, meditation, a simple break, or a prayer.

Sacred Sources

Rav Y'hudah said in the name of Rav: A mourner on the first day of their mourning is prohibited from eating of their own bread. (Babylonian Talmud, *Mo-eid Katan* 27b)

There is a marvelous custom in the Jewish mourning ritual called *s'udat havraah*, the meal of replenishment. On returning from the cemetery, the mourner is not supposed to take food for himself (or to serve others). Other people have to feed him, symbolizing the way the community rallies around him to sustain him and to try to fill the emptiness in his world. (Harold S. Kushner, *When Bad Things Happen to Good People*, p. 133)

- Most of us have people or institutions in our lives that are ready to support us when we need support. Who or which institutions have provided support to you in the last weeks and months? Who provided food? Who nourished you in different ways?
- Jewish tradition makes sure that our mourners feel cared for and safe upon returning from the cemetery to an entirely changed reality. What and who has given you a sense of safety and care since you had to bury your loved one?
- You might find that you are experiencing moments of strength again. When you experience such a moment the next time, ask yourself: Whom can I nourish with this strength? Am I ready to give again?

Poetry and Prayer

Let Evening Come
Jane Kenyon

Let the light of late afternoon
shine through chinks in the barn, moving
up the bales as the sun moves down.

Let the cricket take up chafing
as a woman takes up her needles
and her yarn. Let evening come.

Let dew collect on the hoe abandoned
in long grass. Let the stars appear
and the moon disclose her silver horn.

Let the fox go back to its sandy den.
Let the wind die down. Let the shed
go black inside. Let evening come.

To the bottle in the ditch, to the scoop
in the oats, to air in the lung
let evening come.

Let it come, as it will, and don't
be afraid. God does not leave us
comfortless, so let evening come.

Kaddish and Mourning Prayers

See page 175.

Week 3

Asher Yatzar
Text: Morning Blessings, *Birchot HaShachar*
English Lyrics and Music: Dan Nichols

I thank You for my life, body and soul.
Help me realize I'm beautiful and whole.
I'm perfect the way I am
And a little broken too.
I will live each day as a gift I give to you.

בָּרוּךְ אַתָּה, יְיָ, רוֹפֵא כָל בָּשָׂר וּמַפְלִיא לַעֲשׂוֹת.
Baruch atah, Adonai, rofei chol basar umafli laasot. (2x)
Blessed are You, Adonai, the wondrous healer of all flesh.

Kavanah

When in mourning, we often have no choice but to share our emotions with others. We end up sharing our brokenness, our less-than-perfect coping mechanism, our swollen faces after crying, our helpless search for words.

Have a look at yourself in the mirror. Has the time of mourning changed your face? Your eyes? Where in your body do you feel differently than you felt before the loss? Where in your body does the memory of your beloved person dwell?

Sacred Sources

So often, when I meet with a family after a death and before a funeral service, they will ask me, "Do we really need to sit *shiva*, to have all those people crowding into our living room? Couldn't we just ask them to leave us alone?" My response is, "No, letting people into your home, into your grief, is exactly what you need now. You need to share with them, to talk to them, to let them comfort you. You need to be reminded that you are still alive, and part of a world of life." (Harold S. Kushner, *When Bad Things Happen to Good People*, p. 133)

- We often want to hide from the world when we feel broken, sad, and full of pain. Yet, Jewish mourning customs challenge us to sit with others exactly at those times. How do you experience the company of others when you feel broken? How does sharing your brokenness change your experience of it?
- Life itself does not stop when our personal lives are turned upside down. Think about your own social universe. What has happened since you experienced your loss? Who moved? Whose work situation changed? Who else died? Were babies born? Did anyone get divorced? Has anyone graduated or retired?
- We all are, to varying degrees, social creatures. Reach out to a friend, ask how they are, and just listen to their response.

Poetry and Prayer

Mourning to Dancing
Devon A. Spier

What does it take to turn mourning to dancing?

First, a reaching forward.
A subtle movement out of the slump of our shiva chair (not quite upright, but still).

Then, the planting of our feet on the ground.
"Yes," we are here and grounded in the roots of divine justice.
It is now possible to stand.

Though the whispers of fate and even the Angel of Death
Tell us to stay a while.
To reject words of consolation for the heaviness of our sorrow.
Though they would have us look away from ourselves and all life,
We face the dark.

And somewhere, a prism of light forms.
We can barely make it out.
But when our vision and we, too, are ready
We see it as bright as day:

"Arise."

Arise in the presence of friends.
Arise and leave behind the tear and the tearing.
Arise and make those first few steps among the living.

And though we stand up and sit down,
Agonize over what we are able to do and not do,
Individual acts of mind, body, and soul
Will lead us to give up the grief and ignite our dry bones.

And one of these days when we least expect it, we will find
ourselves dancing.

Kaddish and Mourning Prayers

See page 175.

Week 4

Song

Mozi's *Nigun* (*Ana B'cho-ach*)
Text: *Ana B'cho-ach—Kabbalat Shabbat* Liturgy
Music: Joey Weisenberg

אָנָּא בְּכֹחַ גְּדֻלַּת יְמִינְךָ. תַּתִּיר צְרוּרָה
קַבֵּל רִנַּת עַמְּךָ. שַׂגְּבֵנוּ טַהֲרֵנוּ נוֹרָא.

Ana b'cho-ach g'dulat y'mincha. Tatir tz'rurah,
kabeil rinat amcha. Sagveinu tahareinu nora.

We beg You with the strength and greatness of Your right arm.
Untangle our knotted fate,
Accept Your people's song. Elevate and purify us, Awesome One.

Kavanah

For some of us, Jewish texts and melodies feel like well-worn clothes—soft and comfortable. For others, they are fresh, crisp, and new.

Go back to one of the songs that filled you with energy, gratitude, and a sense of being alive. Listen to it again. And again.

Sacred Sources

> Great is Torah for it gives life to those who practice it, in this world and in the world-to-come, as it is said: "They are life unto those that find them, and healing for their whole bodies" (Proverbs 4:22). (*Pirkei Avot* 6:7)

- Not everyone finds comfort in ancient texts. However, sometimes those texts get set to music and then slowly find their way into our souls. Think back to the days, weeks, and months of mourning that have passed. Which texts spoke to you instantly? Which words and sentences turned into steady companions?

- What might "practicing Torah" have meant for the author(s) of Proverbs? What does it mean to you?
- When we read ancient texts together with others, we enter into a multigenerational conversation. When have you learned from the past and from Jewish tradition, and when have you learned to distance yourself from a part of it?

Poetry and Prayer

Your Name: Meditation at Dusk

Alden Solovy

God of our ancestors,
Your name is Peace.
Your name is Justice.
Your name is Mercy.

God of life,
Your name is Compassion.
Your name is Love.
Your name is Hope.

God of blessing,
Your name is Truth.
Your name is Wisdom.
Your name is Righteousness.

God of our fathers,
God of our mothers,
Your name is in my heart
And before my eyes.

Blessed are You, Adonai,
Your name shines throughout Creation.

Kaddish and Mourning Prayers

See page 175.

Week 5

Song

Nachamu
Text: Isaiah 40:1
English Lyrics and Music: Elana Arian

נַחֲמוּ נַחֲמוּ עַמִּי יֹאמַר אֱלֹהֵיכֶם.
Nachamu, nachamu ami yomar Eloheichem.

Comfort us, comfort us in our wilderness,
Comfort us as we struggle to take care of one another;
Comfort us, comfort us in our wilderness,
Comfort us as we struggle with this world.

Kavanah

Many of us know Jewish prayer only in the form of the set prayers in our prayer books. Yet, Jewish tradition knows of many kinds of prayers.

Find a place in your home. Settle down. Bring tea—or not. Bring a pillow—or not. Close your eyes—or not. Speak to yourself—or to God. Listen to the words that come. And then let them rise.

Sacred Sources

People who pray for miracles usually don't get miracles, any more than children who pray for bicycles, good grades, or boyfriends get them as a result of praying. But people who pray for courage, for strength to bear the unbearable, for the grace to remember what they have left instead of what they have lost, very often find their prayers answered. (Harold S. Kushner, *When Bad Things Happen to Good People*, p. 138)

- Think about your own prayer experiences: at synagogues, out in nature, or in your home; in community or by yourself; following a prayer book or making it up on the spot. When have those experiences felt whole and holy to you? When not?

- Do you know a prayer, even if it is just one sentence, that you might want to say more regularly? What is it? How might saying a prayer or mantra change certain moments for you, moments like waking up, going to bed, leaving for work, preparing a meal, sitting down with friends and family, seeing something beautiful, or feeling alone?
- Jewish prayer is often driven by notions of gratitude and praise—as well as pleas for strength and health, and confessions. Which of these modes comes most naturally to you these days?

Poetry and Prayer

Prayer Invites
Rabbi Abraham Joshua Heschel

Prayer invites
God's presence to suffuse our spirits,
God's will to prevail in our lives.
Prayer may not bring water to parched fields,
nor mend a broken bridge,
nor rebuild a ruined city.
But prayer can water an arid soul,
mend a broken heart,
rebuild a weakened will.

בָּרוּךְ אַתָּה יְיָ מְחַיֵּה הַמֵּתִים.
Baruch atah, Adonai, m'chayeih hameitim.
Blessed are You, Adonai, who revives the dead.

Kaddish and Mourning Prayers

See page 175.

Week 6

Song

B'yado
Text: From *Adon Olam*
Music: Craig Taubman

בְּיָדוֹ אַפְקִיד רוּחִי, בְּעֵת אִישַׁן וְאָעִירָה,
וְעִם רוּחִי גְּוִיָּתִי, יְיָ לִי וְלֹא אִירָא.

B'yado afkid ruchi, b'eit ishan v'a-irah,
v'im ruchi g'viyati, Adonai li v'lo ira.

My soul I give to You, my spirit in Your care.
Draw me near, I shall not fear.
Hold me in Your hand.

Kavanah

Maybe you have heard, over the last weeks and months, sayings and sentences that presume a certain form of afterlife: "They are waiting for you," "They are looking down at you," or "One day, you will be together again."

Take a moment. Try not to judge yourself. Nothing is childish; nothing is stupid; nothing needs to be proven. Right now, what is your sense of your beloved's presence in your life and in the world in general?

Sacred Sources

The following two texts offer very different takes on the ways in which hope can help you find comfort during your mourning period. First is a midrash about Joshua's response to the death of his teacher and leader Moses. Here, we see God reminding Joshua that he is not the only one mourning Moses's death. God, too, is in mourning. God doesn't directly instruct Joshua to stop mourning. Rather, God tells Joshua that Moses is assured a place in the world-to-come.

The second text is a passage from The World to Come, *a contemporary novel by Dara Horn. Here, one of the central characters is telling her daughter her way of understanding the world-to-come as the meeting place between those who have died and those who have yet to be born.*

> When Moses died, Joshua cried and screamed and mourned for him many days, until the Holy One, blessed be God, said to him, "Joshua, how long will you mourn him? Does his death affect you alone? Does his death not also affect Me? For I have been in mourning from the day he died, as it is said: 'And the Lord of Hosts called for crying and lamenting, etc.' [Isaiah 22:12]. And, what is more, he is assured of life in the world-to-come, as it is said: 'Behold, you shall lie down with your ancestors' [Deuteronomy 31:16]." (*Sifrei D'varim* 305:6 on Deuteronomy 31:16)

> I believe that when people die, they go to the same place as all the people who haven't yet been born. That's why it's called the world to come, because that's where they make the new souls for the future. And the reward when good people die"—her mother paused, swallowed, paused again—"the reward when good people die is that they get to help make the people in their families who haven't been born yet. They pick out what kinds of traits they want the new people to have—they give them all the raw material of their souls, like their talents and their brains and their potential. Of course it's up to the new ones, once they're born, what they'll use and what they won't, but that's what everyone who dies is doing, I think. They get to decide what kind of people the new ones might be able to become." She brushed a loose bit of hair away from her face. "That's why your children will be lucky, Sara, because Dad is going to help make them who they're going to be—just like my father helped make you." (Dara Horn, *The World to Come*, p. 124)

- What do you think is the purpose of God's assurance of Moses having a place in the world-to-come for Joshua? How could Joshua possibly hear God's words?
- How do you understand Dara Horn's description of what happens in the world-to-come?
- In what ways, if any, do these two descriptions help you to think about what happens after death?

Poetry and Prayer

The Archaeologist of the Soul

Rabbi Karyn D. Kedar

I suppose that the archaeologist
delights in brokenness.
Shards are proof of life.
Though a vessel, whole, but dusty
and rare, is also good.

I suppose that the archaeologist
does not agonize over the charred
lines of destruction signifying
a war, a conquest, a loss, a fire,
or a complete collapse.
The blackened layer
seared upon the balk
is discovery.

So why do I mourn,
and shiver,
and resist?
Why do I weep
as I dig deeper
and deeper still?
Dust, dirt,
buckets of rubble,
brokenness,
a fire or two,
shattered layers
of a life that
rebuilds upon
the discarded,
the destroyed,
and then
the reconstructed,
only to break again,
and deeper still,
shards upon shards,
layers upon layers.

If you look carefully,
the earth reveals its secrets.
So does the soul,
and the cell,
and the sinew,
and the thought,
and the wisp of memory,
and the laugh,
and the cry,
and the heart,
that seeks its deepest truth,
digging down,
down to bedrock.

Rock bottom they call it,
and in Hebrew,
the Mother Rock.

God of grace,
teach me
that the layers
of brokenness
create a whole.

Kaddish and Mourning Prayers

See page 175.

COMFORT

Week 7

Song

Nachamu
Text: Isaiah 40:1
English Text and Music: Elana Arian

נַחֲמוּ נַחֲמוּ עַמִּי יֹאמַר אֱלֹהֵיכֶם.
Nachamu, nachamu ami yomar Eloheichem.

Comfort us, comfort us in our wilderness,
Comfort us as we struggle to take care of one another;
Comfort us, comfort us in our wilderness,
Comfort us as we struggle with this world.

Kavanah

Most of us avoid thinking about our own death. Yet, we also love to plan for the years ahead; we have bucket lists, life goals, and career goals. We dream of seeing graduations, weddings, and newborn babies.

Settle into your heart and mind for a second. What do you want to accomplish before you die? What will make your life truly yours? What will fill you with a sense of ease thinking about its end?

Sacred Sources

In the days to come,
the Mount of the Eternal's House
stands firm above the mountains
and towers above the hills;
and all the nations
shall gaze on it with joy.
And the many people shall go and say:
"Come,
let us go to the Mount of the Eternal,
to the House of the God of Jacob,

that God may instruct us in God's ways,
and that we may walk in God's paths."
For instruction shall come forth from Zion,
the word of the Eternal from Jerusalem.
(Isaiah 2:2–3)

- The prophet Isaiah paints a picture of the messianic future in which all of us live in dignity and justice. Close your eyes for a second: What are two characteristics of a perfect world for you?
- Isaiah's world has a clear center: God's Temple. What is the center of your world? Which places give you a sense of arrival and being home?
- "God's path" is a path of dignity, justice, and integrity. It gives those who follow it a sense of calm. When do you feel like you walk in God's path? When less so?

Poetry and Prayer

Elijah de Vidas, translated by Lawrence Fine

Shekhinah [God's Presence] does not reside except in a heart which is contrite. . . . A person must prepare a lovely dwelling place in one's heart for the *Shekhinah*. This means that an individual has to act humbly and avoid losing one's temper. For when one behaves in an arrogant manner, the *Shekhinah* takes flight and a handmaiden rules in her mistress' place.

Kaddish and Mourning Prayers

See page 175.

RESILIENCE

How I Can Still Feel Close to You

Week 1

Song

Yah Ana
Text: Y'hudah HaLevi
Music: Dan Nichols and Cantor Ellen Dreskin

יָהּ אָנָה אֶמְצָאֲךָ?
מְקוֹמְךָ נַעֲלֶה וְנֶעְלָם.
וְאָנָה לֹא אֶמְצָאֲךָ?
כְּבוֹדְךָ מָלֵא עוֹלָם.

דָּרַשְׁתִּי קִרְבָתְךָ,
בְּכָל לִבִּי קְרָאתִיךָ
וּבְצֵאתִי לִקְרָאתְךָ
לִקְרָאתִי מְצָאתִיךָ.

Where might I go to find You,
Exalted, Hidden One?
Yet where would I not go to find You,
Everpresent, Eternal One?

My heart cries out to You:
Please draw near to me.
The moment I reach out for You,
I find You reaching in for me.

Kavanah

Each of us carries with us a sense of our heritage—the heritage of our families, religious communities, and maybe even nations or cities.

What are the memories and stories that give you a sense of direction? Whose mission are you carrying forth with your own life?

Sacred Sources

Joseph adjured Israel's children, saying, "God will surely take care of you; bring my bones up from this place!" Joseph died aged 110 years. They embalmed him and he was put into a coffin in Egypt. (Genesis 50:25)

- Jewish tradition forbids embalming. And yet, the story of Joseph's death and embalming is strangely comforting. By means of embalming and keeping his body, the people of Israel were able to feel close to Joseph, even after his death. What are objects and places that carry the memory of the deceased for you?
- Joseph leaves his people a mission: to watch over his embalmed body and to bring it home one day. Many people die without stating such an explicit last wish. What would be a mission your loved one might have left you?
- By "listening" to the wishes of our deceased loved ones, we avoid a sense of radical loss and rupture. Yet, some of the missions and wishes we inherit might also caught damage. What might such a potentially damaging inheritance be for you? How can you let go?

Poetry and Prayer

We Have Always Been
Rabbi Dave Yedid

I look back into history,
pouring over our texts, sacred and profane,
searching
for some kind of opening
where I can see myself, where I can see us.

I search
and find
rejection from our communities and leaders,
our existence hidden, shamed, criminalized, excommunicated,
jailed, killed.

I keep searching
and catch a glimpse
of our vitality, our desire, our love, our bliss, our rebellion,
our chosen family.

In these glimpses I see a sliver of light
pouring out of the opening.
I sprint toward it—our past, our present, our future—
and, with all my might, break the door off its hinges.

I pant, breathless, on the other side.
I want to scream, but instead, I whisper: "*We are here. We are here.*"

We have always been.

Kaddish and Mourning Prayers

See page 175.

Week 2

Song

Olam Chesed Yibaneh
Text: Psalm 89
English Lyrics and Music: Rabbi Menachem Creditor

עוֹלָם חֶסֶד יִבָּנֶה.
Olam chesed yibaneh.

I will build this world from love,
And you must build this world from love.
And if we build this world from love,
Then God will build this world from love.

Kavanah

Philosopher Arnold Toynbee, in his essay "Reflections on My Own Death," has stated that true love might be proved by the wish of a person to outlive his loved one, so that the loved one is spared the anguish of grief.

Rich or poor, young or old, no one is exempt from the devastating effects of grief. All mourn. All suffer.

Everyone who lives a full life must, at some time or another, live with an empty chair. Whether the chair you live with belonged to a parent or spouse, a child or lover, a best friend or relative, it is empty now, and its emptiness represents a task for you. To accomplish this task is to become accustomed to living with that empty chair. When you no longer fear it or revere it, but simply accept it, you will know that you have completed your grief work. (Roberta Temes, *Living With an Empty Chair: A Guide through Grief*, p. 93)

Close your eyes. Picture the person you loved doing something they loved to do. Smile at them. Savor that memory.

Sacred Sources

Let me be a seal upon your heart,
Like the seal upon your hand.
For love is fierce as death,

Passion is mighty is Sheol;
Its darts are darts of fire,
A blazing flame.
(Song of Songs 8:6)

Love is not changed by Death, and nothing is lost and all in the end is harvest. (Edith Sitwell, "Eurydice," from *Collected Poems of Edith Sitwell*, p. 263)

- We do not know in what form or whether loved ones continue to live after their death. We only know what they leave behind. How does the love and companionship you shared live on in your current life, without them? How do you experience the traces of your love?
- Remember a promise you once made to the person you lost, be it explicit or implicit. How can you live this promise today?
- You may have already discovered that your ability to love is not diminished by the death of your loved one. Who are the people to whom you give your love now? Where do you find reciprocity?

Poetry and Prayer

Comfort Animal

Joy Ladin

Comfort, comfort my people . . .
—Isaiah 40:1

A voice says, "Your punishment has ended."
You never listen to that voice. You really suck
at being comforted.

Another voice says, "Cry."
That voice *always* gets your attention,
keeps you thinking

about withered flowers and withering grass
and all the ways you're like them.
Hard to argue with that.

Death tramples you, an un-housebroken pet
trailing prints and broken stems,
pooping anxiety, PTSD, depression.

It's better to be animal than vegetable
but best of all is to be spirit
flying first or maybe business class

with your emotional support animal, your body,
curled in your lap, soaring with you
above the sense of loss you've mistaken

for the closest to God you can get.
You want to cry? Cry about that.
Who do you think created

the animals to whom you turn for comfort,
dogs, miniature horses, monkeys, ferrets,
hungers you know how to feed,

fears you know how to quiet?
I form them, fur them,
it's my warmth radiating from their bodies,

my love that answers
the love you lavish upon them.
Your deserts and desolations

are highways I travel,
smoothing your broken places,
arranging stars and constellations

to light your wilderness.
Sometimes I play the shepherd;
sometimes I play the lamb;

sometimes I appear as death,
which makes it hard to remember
that I am the one who assembled your atoms,

who crowned your dust with consciousness.
I take you everywhere,
which is why, wherever you go, I'm there,

keeping you hydrated, stroking your hair,
laughing when you chase your tail,
gathering you to my invisible breasts

more tenderly than any mother.
You're right—you never asked for this. I'm the reason
your valleys are being lifted up,

the source of your life laid bare.
Mine is the voice that decrees—
that begs—your anguish to end.

When you suffer, I suffer.
Comfort me
by being comforted.

Kaddish and Mourning Prayers

See page 175.

Week 3

Song

L'cha Amar Libi
Text: adapted from Psalm 27:8
Music: Nava Tehila (Yoel Sykes)

לְךָ אָמַר לִבִּי בַּקְּשׁוּ פָנָי אֶת פָּנֶיךָ יְיָ אֲבַקֵּשׁ . . .
L'cha amar libi bakshu fanai et panecha Adonai avakeish . . .
In Your behalf, my heart says: "Seek My face!"

Kavanah

Death is a life-changing encounter. Once we come into close contact with it, our sense of self is altered forever. Often, it takes us years to understand completely how it happened, but the death of a person close to us changes the dynamics in our families and communities.

Take a moment to compare the life you lived before your beloved's death to the life you are living now. What or who is slowly filling the void? When and where does your life feel marked by their absence? What is the same? What is different? How so?

Sacred Sources

> Let me suggest that the bad things that happen to us in our lives do not have a meaning when they happen to us. They don't happen for any good reason which would cause us to accept them willingly. But we can give them a meaning. We can redeem these tragedies from senselessness by imposing meaning on them. The question we should be asking is not, "Why did this happen to me? What did I do to deserve this?" That is really in an unanswerable, pointless question. A better question would be, "Now that this has happened to me, what am I going to do about it?" (Harold S. Kushner, *When Bad Things Happen to Good People*, p. 149)

- Often, death leaves us without answers. Why now? Why this way? Why them? In spite of knowing better, we cannot always simply ignore those questions. How can you help yourself to live with the unknown, even the unacceptable?

- In better moments, we might be able to take the second step—as Harold Kushner recommends—and leave the "why" in favor of "and now what?" It might be difficult to discern the new form of your life immediately after you lose someone at its center. How can you make sure that what keeps you busy is not mere distraction, but the tender, slow beginning of a life that is different and new?
- Sometimes, if we lose someone we love in tragic ways, we might be tempted to dedicate the rest of our lives to making up for this loss. We dedicate our time and resources to do what the deceased might have wanted to do if they were still alive. But this is not our mission; it was theirs. Each of us has our own mission. How can you make sure not to live in the shadow of death?

Poetry and Prayer

A Mourner's *Kaddish*
Trisha Arlin

Layer Upon layer of attempts to describe the Indescribable.
We cannot help but be separate,
We cannot help but be part of the One.
It is our holy dialectic
In the face of the unknown
And thus our need for
A Name that will describe
A Name that will explain
A Name that will make it easy.
This is not easy.

But how do we name the Un-nameable?
We can but try.
Bless this endeavor;
It has made us so creative.
Bless the Eternal and the Glorious,

The Holy Wholeness,
And let us say, Amen.

It makes us happy to think about God.
Overarching and unseen.

We have absolutely no idea what the truth is,
But we are blessed with this burden
Because we need to describe what cannot be described,
Because we need structure in the face of the vast mysteries,
Because we go on and on and on.
And then, one day we don't.
Blessed One-ness.

We pray, these are requests for meaning despite our doubts,
Despite our fears,
Despite the loss of love and loved ones.

May these prayers be answered,
As unlikely as that may be,
You never know.
And let us say, Amen.

And may the Un-nameable be sanctified
And the Names we have invented to name the Un-nameable
be sanctified
And may The Name we invented to name the names we
invented for the Un-nameable be sanctified.
Layer Upon Layer of attempts to describe the Indescribable,
Those layers allow us to touch the awesome truth
And still be safe.
May our creations flourish and survive our limitations.

Bless The Name of the Names of the Un-nameable
Now
Until
Then.
Layer Upon Layer
May all our prayers be understood,
And let us say, Amen

Blessed One-ness.
However we understand this on any given day,
Making peace and
Sustaining holy completion
For us, through us.
For each other
And all the world,

And let us say, Amen.

Kaddish and Mourning Prayers

See page 175.

Week 4

Song

Yah Ana
Text: Y'hudah HaLevi
Music: Dan Nichols and Cantor Ellen Dreskin

יָהּ אָנָה אֶמְצָאֲךָ?
מְקוֹמְךָ נַעֲלֶה וְנֶעְלָם.
וְאָנָה לֹא אֶמְצָאֲךָ?
כְּבוֹדְךָ מָלֵא עוֹלָם.

דָּרַשְׁתִּי קִרְבָתְךָ,
בְּכָל לִבִּי קְרָאתִיךָ
וּבְצֵאתִי לִקְרָאתְךָ
לִקְרָאתִי מְצָאתִיךָ.

Where might I go to find You,
Exalted, Hidden One?
Yet where would I not go to find You,
Everpresent, Eternal One?

My heart cries out to You:
Please draw near to me.
The moment I reach out for You,
I find You reaching in for me.

Kavanah

Each of us is the sum of our past, and the pasts of our forefathers and foremothers; stories and expectations surrounding us; genetic inheritances; education and personal experiences; love and pain . . .

Close your eyes for a moment. In what ways do you carry the person you lost with you? What are the gifts they left you? In what ways have they changed you forever?

Sacred Sources

I will give them, in My House
And within My walls,
A monument and a name....
I will give them an everlasting name
Which shall not perish.
(Isaiah 56:5)

Forgetfulness leads to exile, while remembrance is the secret of redemption. (Baal Shem Tov, the founder of Chasidism)

- What do you think the Baal Shem Tov meant by this statement? What kind of exile comes from forgetting? How does remembering bring about redemption?
- How can you give the memory of your loved one a place? How can you make sure that people close to you will share your memories and stories about them and remember their name?
- Our memories spin a fine net of connection between those who are dead and those who are alive—and even the ones not born yet. Over generations, and sometimes within one generation, even our DNA itself is changed by the experiences of our past—and therefore, the experiences of preceding generations. In what ways is your life, your opinions and preferences, your instincts and needs, a monument to memory—and maybe also a way to redemption?

Poetry and Prayer

On your journey you will come
Muriel Rukeyser

On your journey you will come to a time of waking.
The others may be asleep. Or you may be alone.

Immediacy of song moving the titled
Visions of children and the linking stars.

You will begin then to remember. You
Hear the voice relating after late listening.

You remember even falling asleep, or a dream of sleep.
For now the song is given and you remember.

At every clear waking you have known this song,
The cities of this music identified

By the white springs of singing, and their fountains
Reflected in windows, in all the human eyes.

The wishes, the need growing. The song growing.

Kaddish and Mourning Prayers

See page 175.

Week 5

Song

L'cha Amar Libi
Text: adapted from Psalm 27:8
Music: Nava Tehila (Yoel Sykes)

לְךָ אָמַר לִבִּי בַּקְּשׁוּ פָנָי אֶת פָּנֶיךָ יְיָ אֲבַקֵּשׁ . . .
L'cha amar libi bakshu fanai et panecha Adonai avakeish . . .
In Your behalf, my heart says: "Seek My face!"

Kavanah

Grief is a natural reaction to the loss of a loved one. It would be strange if you didn't live through and with it. It is normal for grief to come and go; to sometimes be less intense and sometimes be overwhelming. However, grief itself can also take on a weight that prevents us from thinking clearly, from remembering, even from taking care of our own responsibilities.

Ask yourself: "Am I good to myself?" Ask yourself: "Am I good to others?" Ask yourself: "How heavily does my grief weigh on me?" Ask yourself: "How heavily does my grief weigh on others?"

Sacred Sources

> Whenever the evil spirit . . . came upon Saul, David would take the lyre and play it; Saul would find relief and feel better, and the evil spirit would leave him. (I Samuel 16:23)

- In the story of King Saul and David, David—a young shepherd and musician—is able to give the anxious and restless King Saul some rest by playing his music. Do you have musicians or a source of music in your life that have a similar effect on you? What or who are they?
- At times, grief and fear can become "evil spirits." Instead of helping us to work our way through our ungraspable loss, they turn into obstacles that keep us from understanding and feeling calm. We feel like we are drowning or literally

losing our minds. If you encounter such an evil spirit, who or what helps you to break the spell and find relief?

- The story of Saul and David also makes it clear that the evil spirit keeps on returning to Saul. Saul's anxiety and depression come in waves, similar to our own waves of grief. Think about the waves you are now already familiar with: What is their rhythm? What is their strength? Do they bring you closer to the dead? Do they distance you from life?

Poetry and Prayer

Hope
Lisel Mueller

It hovers in dark corners
before the lights are turned on,
it shakes sleep from its eyes
and drops from mushroom gills,
it explodes in the starry heads
of dandelions turned sages,
it sticks to the wings of green angels
that sail from the tops of maples.
It sprouts in each occluded eye
of the many-eyed potato,
it lives in each earthworm segment
surviving cruelty,
it is the motion that runs
from the eyes to the tail of a dog,
it is the mouth that inflates the lungs
of the child that has just been born.
It is the singular gift
we cannot destroy in ourselves,
the argument that refutes death,
the genius that invents the future,
all we know of God.
It is the serum which makes us swear
not to betray one another;
it is in this poem, trying to speak.

Kaddish and Mourning Prayers

See page 175.

Week 6

Song

Olam Chesed Yibaneh
Text: Psalm 89:3
English Lyrics and Music: Rabbi Menachem Creditor

עוֹלָם חֶסֶד יִבָּנֶה.
Olam chesed yibaneh.

I will build this world from love,
And you must build this world from love.
And if we build this world from love,
Then God will build this world from love.

Kavanah

All of us build together the world in which we live.

What does it mean to you "to build from love"? When in your life do you have a strong sense of building from love? Can your grieving be, at least in a certain way, an act of building from love?

Sacred Sources

Waking up from his sleep, Jacob said, "Truly, the Eternal is in this place, and I did not know it!" . . . Rising early that morning, Jacob took the stone that he had put under his head and set it up as a monument. He then poured oil on its top. (Genesis 28:16, 18)

- In a dream, Jacob has the vision of the ladder connecting the place where he went to sleep to heaven. When do you have a sense of connection to something bigger than you?
- What does the biblical image of "setting up a stone as a monument and pouring oil on its top" mean to you? How would you honor a place in which you found wholeness, holiness, hope, and vision?
- The relationships we build throughout our lives, the music we make, our words, our thoughts, our actions . . . all of

these turn into "monuments" in time, and sometimes also in place. How can you revisit the monuments the deceased left you, and how can you "pour oil on their top"?

Poetry and Prayer

Life and Death

Rabbi Harold M. Schulweis

When dying is over, a different kind of memory takes over.
Not the memory that is obituary.
Not the memory that records the past indiscriminately.
But an active memory that sifts through the ashes of the past
to retrieve isolated moments and that gives heart to the future.
That memory is an act of resurrection.
It raises up from oblivious the glories of forgotten years.

Even the memories of failure, the recollections
of frustration and regret are precious.
Broken memories are like the tablets Moses shattered,
placed lovingly in the holy Ark of remembrance.
Memories are saved, those immaterial, disembodied ghosts
that endure.

What is life after death?
Pointers, ensigns, marking places
that raise us up to life and give us a changed heart.
Perhaps a life lived differently, better, wiser, stronger
than before.
What is left after death? The life of the survivor.

Kaddish and Mourning Prayers

See page 175.

Week 7

Song

Ozi V'zimrat Yah
Text: Psalm 118:14; Exodus 15:2
Music: Rabbi Shefa Gold

עָזִּי וְזִמְרַת יָהּ וַיְהִי לִי לִישׁוּעָה.
Ozi v'zimrat Yah vay'hi li lishuah.
My strength balanced with the Song of God will be my salvation.

Kavanah

God is sometimes called "the Source of life." Life, for us humans, often comes to us in the form of food and drink, air and rest.

Just today, what were some of the most life-giving things you did? How did you experience them—and does your memory of them change answering this question?

Sacred Sources

> I have already mentioned that the tastes of Jewish foods often trigger my memories of family members, friends, and special happy and sometimes sad occasions. I imagine that the reader of this essay can also recall a time when the smell or taste of a . . . food transported them back in time. (Melanie Cole Goldberg, "Experiencing God While Making Jewish Food," in *Because My Soul Longs for You: Integrating Theology into Our Lives*, eds. Edwin C. Goldberg and Elaine S. Zecher, p. 40.)

- Sometimes it is a piece of music, sometimes it is a word or saying, sometimes it is a certain object—and often, it is a taste or smell that triggers the strongest memories in us. What was your beloved's favorite food? When and how would they like to eat it?
- Decide on a time of year when you will savor your beloved's favorite dish. (It doesn't matter whether you like it or not!) Mark this occasion in your calendar.

- What are the foods you would like people to associate with you? How can you share those with others more often?

Poetry and Prayer

Reflection before *Kaddish*

Rabbi Richard Levy

It is hard to sing of oneness when the world is not
complete,
when those who once brought wholeness to our life
have gone,
and naught but memory can fill the emptiness their
passing leaves behind.

But memory can tell us only what we were, in company
with those we loved;
it cannot help us find what each of us, alone, must now
become.
Yet no one is really alone:
those who live no more, echo still within our thoughts
and words,
and what they did is part of what we have become.

We do our best homage to our dead when we live our
lives more fully,
even in the shadow of our loss.
For each of our lives is worth the life of the whole world;
in each one is the breath of the Ultimate One.
In affirming the One, we affirm the worth of each one
whose life, now ended, brought us closer to the Source
of life,
in whose unity no one is alone and every life finds purpose.

Kaddish and Mourning Prayers

See page 175.

ACCEPTANCE

Honoring You, Honoring Myself

Week 1

Song

Those Who Sow
Text: Psalm 126:5
English Lyrics and Music: Debbie Friedman

הַזֹּרְעִים בְּדִמְעָה בְּרִנָּה יִקְצֹרוּ.

Hazorim b'dimah b'rinah yiktzoru.

Those who sow, who sow in tears
Will reap in joy, will reap in joy!
Those who sow, who sow in tears
Will reap, will reap in joy!

It's the song of the dreamer
From the dark place it grows
Like a flower in the desert
The oasis of our souls
Come back, come back where we belong
You who hear our longing sighs [*or:* cries]
Our mouths, our lips are filled with song.

Kavanah

This may be a jarring question for some but it is worth reflection: How much did you pay for your mourning? Or: How much do you think the people in charge of the funeral paid? What else do you know of that costs that much?

Take a moment to contemplate that question. It is impossible to place a fiscal value on the death of a loved one. Yet, the reality is that we must pay for the costs. How does this obligation sit with you? Where might it provide a sense of comfort or acceptance?

Sacred Sources

Sara died in Kiriat-Arba (that is, Hebron) in the land of Canaan, and Abraham proceeded to mourn for Sarah and to bewail her. Then Abraham rose up from upon his dead [wife], and spoke to the

> Hittites, saying, "I am a foreigner living for a long time among you; sell me a graveside among you, but I may bury my dead here." . . . Afterward, Abraham buried his wife Sarah in the cave of the field of Machpelah—facing Mamre (that is, Hebron)—in the land of Canaan. (Genesis 23:2–4, 23:19)

> Likewise, at first burying the dead was more difficult for the relatives than the actual death, because it was customary to bury the dead in expensive shrouds which the poor could not afford. The problem grew to the point that relatives would sometimes abandon the corpse and run away. This lasted until Rabban Gamliel . . . left instructions that he be buried in linen garments. And the people adopted this practice and had themselves buried in linen garments. Rav Pappa said: And nowadays, everyone follows the practice of burying the dead in plain hemp garments that cost only a dinar. (Babylonian Talmud, *Mo-eid Katan* 27b)

- Jewish tradition asks us to bury our dead in a Jewish cemetery, where their graves will remain untouched forever. We make sure that we have the right to do so and lay our dead to an "eternal rest." What does this tradition tell you about the dignity of the deceased in Jewish tradition?
- However, it also became the custom to bury our dead in the simplest garments and wooden coffins. What does that custom tell you about the dignity of the mourners?
- Death and mourning, according to Jewish tradition, should not be financial burdens. How do you see this principle unfolding today—and how not? What are contemporary challenges to this principle? How might we overcome those challenges?

ACCEPTANCE

Poetry and Prayer

Prayer for the Dead

Stuart Kestenbaum

The light snow started late last night and continued
all night long while I slept and could hear it occasionally
enter my sleep, where I dreamed my brother
was alive again and possessing the beauty of youth, aware

that he would be leaving again shortly and that is the lesson
of the snow falling and of the seeds of death that are in everything
that is born: we are here for a moment
of a story that is longer than all of us and few of us
remember, the wind is blowing out of someplace
we don't know, and each moment contains rhythms
within rhythms, and if you discover some old piece
of your own writing, or an old photograph,
you may not remember that it was you and even if it was
once you,
it's not you now, not this moment that the synapses fire
and your hands move to cover your face in a gesture
of grief and remembrance.

Kaddish and Mourning Prayers

See page 175.

Week 2

Song

Ki Imcha, M'kor Chayim
Text: Psalm 36:10
Music: Rabbi David Zeller, *z"l*

כִּי עִמְּךָ, מְקוֹר חַיִּים; בְּאוֹרְךָ נִרְאֶה אוֹר.
Ki imcha, m'kor chayim; b'orcha nireh or.
For with You is the source of life; in Your light we see light.

Kavanah

Visualize the life of the person you lost. Did they get to do everything they wanted to do? Did they get to say everything they wanted to say?

Take the time to write your own list: What do you want to be able to tell your loved ones before you die? What do you want to do before you die?

Start now.

Sacred Sources

> And [Jacob] gave them a charge, saying, "When I am gathered to my people, bury me with my ancestors—in the cave that is in the field of Ephron the Hittite, in the cave that is in the field of Machpelah, facing Mamre, in the land of Canaan, the field that Abraham bought from the Ephron the Hittite as an inalienable gravesite. There they buried Abraham and his wife Sarah, there they buried Isaac and his wife Rebekah, and there I buried Leah. . . . When Jacob was done charging his sons, he drew his feet into the bed; he then breathed his last and was gathered to his people. (Genesis 49:29–31, 33)

- Jacob's death is an example of a process of dying in which the deceased person has the time and the attention of their loved ones to say their final words: words of blessing, of warning, of goodbyes, and of final wishes. Some of his words must have been hard to hear. When in your life did you have to listen to difficult words without being given the chance to react?

- Jacob wishes to be buried with his family. How do you understand that wish? What might be Jacob's motivation?
- Jewish custom warns us not to visit the cemetery too frequently. Instead, we are asked to focus on those who are alive. What does this custom protect us from? What might be a good frequency to visit the grave of your loved one for you?

Poetry and Prayer

Stones

Barbara Leff

At Normandy

Endless rows of white crosses
recall the wineries back home:
vines planted at precise intervals
to insure maximum yield.
Here where there's neither
crop nor profit,
precision gives way to prayer.
Symmetry shifts to surprise:
a single six-sided star
then another, and yet another, scattered
like punctuation marks in a run-on sentence:
a pause to underscore the waste of war.
Without words, we scavenge for stones
spread out to pay respects.
I place a pebble on the grave of one
who at 22 saw things I don't dare imagine,
his name as familiar as my own—
a distant cousin perhaps, or not—
just a soul, like any other, gone
from this earth the length of a lifetime.
I hold tight to the stones
as the grass moves in waves
ripples and curls at the sandy

edge of each gravestone
each part of a unique eco-system
whose journey will continue
long past the end of mine.

Kaddish and Mourning Prayers

See page 175.

Week 3

Song

Those Who Sow
Text: Psalm 126:5
English Lyrics and Music: Debbie Friedman

הַזֹּרְעִים בְּדִמְעָה בְּרִנָּה יִקְצֹרוּ.

Hazorim b'dimah b'rinah yiktzoru.

Those who sow, who sow in tears
Will reap in joy, will reap in joy!
Those who sow, who sow in tears
Will reap, will reap in joy!

It's the song of the dreamer
From the dark place it grows
Like a flower in the desert
The oasis of our souls
Come back, come back where we belong
You who hear our longing sighs [*or:* cries]
Our mouths, our lips are filled with song.

Kavanah

Over the course of the first year of mourning, we learn to live with our memories. We get used to their coming and going; we might even assign them certain times and places.

When do you like to remember your loved one? When do you like to tell others about them? What is the most dominant emotion accompanying your memories?

Sacred Sources

When David saw his servants talking in whispers, David understood that the child was dead. David asked his servants, "Is the child dead?" "Yes," they replied. Thereupon David rose from the ground; he bathed and anointed himself, and he changed his clothes. He went into the House of the Eternal and prostrated himself. Then he went home and asked for food, which they set before him, and he ate. His courtiers asked him, "Why have you acted in this manner? While the child was alive, you fasted and wept; but now that the child is dead, you rise and take food!" He replied, "While the child was still alive, I fasted and wept because I thought, 'Who knows? The Eternal may have pity on me, and the child may live.' But now that he is dead, why should I fast? Can I bring him back again? I shall go to him, but he will never come back to me." (II Samuel 12:19–23)

- The story of the death of David's and Bathsheba's first son is a story that might sound familiar to those of us who have been caring for slowly and sometimes painfully dying relatives and friends. Each day brings new pains, each day brings more exhaustion—to all the people in the room. Death, we sometimes say, can be a relief. Can you understand David's reaction to his son's death—at least in part?
- David's courtiers wonder about David's behavior, and they ask him about it. We are often quick to judge the mourning behavior of others. We wonder if they are done too quickly, if they mourn excessively, if they are having too much fun, if they are depressing others . . . the truth is that every person mourns differently, and that grief has many different faces. What has surprised you about your own needs during this time of mourning?
- David says, "He will never come back to me." In what ways might it be helpful to state the truth so bluntly? When is it appropriate? When not?

Poetry and Prayer

Birdwings

Rumi, translated by Coleman Barks

Your grief for what you've lost lifts a mirror
up to where you're bravely working.

Expecting the worst, you look, and instead,
here's the joyful face you've been waiting to see.

Your hand opens and closes and opens and closes.
If it were always a fist or always stretched open,
you would be paralyzed.

Your deepest presence is in every small contracting
  and expanding,
the two as beautifully balanced and coordinated
as birdwings.

Kaddish and Mourning Prayers

See page 175.

Week 4

Song

Ki Imcha, M'kor Chayim
Text: Psalm 36:10
Music: Rabbi David Zeller, *z"l*

כִּי עִמְּךָ, מְקוֹר חַיִּים; בְּאוֹרְךָ נִרְאֶה אוֹר.
Ki imcha, m'kor chayim; b'orcha nireh or.
For with You is the source of life; in Your light we see light.

Kavanah

Most of us go through several periods of darkness when we mourn the death of someone dear to us. The Psalmist says, "Surely, the dark will hide me" (Psalm 139:11). Sometimes, the dark provides comfort, sometimes it is a refuge, and other times it may feel like a terrifying prison. Finding light in the midst of loss can be an overwhelming task.

For the Psalmists, light is almost always associated with God. What is a source of light for you?

Sacred Sources

Perish the day on which I was born,
And the night it was announced,
"A male has been conceived!"
(Job 3:3–5)

I looked forward to good fortune, but evil came;
I hoped for light, but darkness came.
(Job 30:26)

Where were you when I laid the earth's foundations?
Speak, if you have understanding. . . .
Have you ever commanded the day to break,
Assigned the dark its place? . . .

Have you penetrated to the sources of the sea,
Or walked in the recesses of the deep?
(Job 38:4, 38:12, 38:16)

The natural world of God's reply to Job, like the water of Iguasso, is unrestrained, turbulent, powerful, joyous, and beautiful. I had noticed this dimension of Job before but had dismissed it as irrelevant to the book's central problematic. I was never able to hold together my indignation at God's refusal to answer Job's question about justice and my love for the language of the "morning star [singing] together," the horse pawing "in the valley, and [exulting] in his strength," and the Behemoth, made as God made us, "eating grass like an ox" (38:7; 39:21; 40:15). But now it strikes me that, much as Job may not want to hear it, this is God's answer to his question. . . . It is not about you or your human standards. The world is about other things entirely: creativity, beauty, diversity, power, energy. . . . The reality is that God's speeches show no concern for fairness, and, in any event, it makes no sense to talk about justice and at the same time assert that God's justice is incomprehensible. (Judith Plaskow in *Goddess and God in the World: Conversations in Embodied Theology*, pp. 188–89)

- Judith Plaskow's theology is an invitation to dive into our wild and beautiful world—without expecting it to fulfill our expectations or to act "justly." Do you recall a moment in which you shared her sense for the beauty and wildness of life itself, in which life delighted you?
- Job, on the other hand, is a good example of someone who looks for justice and falls into despair, realizing that he will not find it in this world. When have you shared Job's feeling of despair and vulnerability?
- Over the course of our lives we might experience times when we feel in control, times when we feel overwhelmed and helpless, and times when trust in God or fate seems to guide our decisions. Which of these is most familiar to you?

Poetry and Prayer

e.e. cummings

i thank You God for most this amazing
day: for the leaping greenly spirits of trees
and a blue true dream of sky; and for everything
which is natural which is infinite which is yes
(i who have died am alive again today,
and this is the sun's birthday; this is the birth
day of life and of love and wings: and of the gay
great happening illimitably earth)
how should tasting touching hearing seeing
breathing any–lifted from the no
of all nothing–human merely being
doubt unimaginable You?
(now the ears of my ears awake and
now the eyes of my eyes are opened)

Kaddish and Mourning Prayers

See page 175.

Week 5

Song

Vaani t'filati

Text: Psalm 69:14

Music: Rabbi Josh Warshawsky and Yael Bettenhausen

וַאֲנִי תְפִלָּתִי לְךָ, יְיָ, עֵת רָצוֹן.
אֱלֹהִים, בְּרָב חַסְדֶּךָ, עֲנֵנִי בֶּאֱמֶת יִשְׁעֶךָ.

Vaani t'filati l'cha, Adonai, eit ratzon.
Elohim, b'rov chasdecha, aneini be-emet yishecha.

As for me, may my prayer come to You, Adonai, at a favorable time. O God, in Your abundant faithfulness, answer me with Your sure deliverance.

Kavanah

When grieving, certain activities might suddenly become painful. Others might bring relief.

What are activities that bring you pain—maybe because they are connected to too many painful or beautiful memories? Which ones bring you joy—possibly for similar reasons?

Sacred Sources

The Sages taught: When the Second Temple was destroyed, there was an increase in the number of ascetics among the Jewish people whose practice was to not eat meat and to not drink wine. Rabbi Y'hoshua joined them to discuss their practice. He said to them, "My children, for what reason do you not eat meat and do you not drink wine?" They said to him, "Shall we eat meat, from which offerings are sacrificed upon the altar, and now the altar has ceased to exist? Shall we drink wine, which is poured as a libation upon the altar, and now the altar has ceased to exist?" Rabbi Y'hoshua said to them, "If so, we will not eat bread either, since the meal-offerings that were offered upon the altar have ceased." They replied, "You are correct. It is possible to subsist with produce." He said to them, "We will not eat produce either, since the bringing of the first fruits have ceased." They replied, "You are correct. We will no longer eat the produce of the seven species from which the first fruits were brought, as it is possible to subsist with other produce." He said to them, "If so, we will not drink water, since the water libation has ceased." They were silent, as they realized that they could not survive without water. (Babylonian Talmud, *Bava Batra* 60b)

- When suffering an enormous loss, we might have a sense that our lives are changed and our happiness is lost forever. Do you recall moments in your life when that was true for you?
- At a later point, when happiness finds its way back to us, we might sometimes feel guilty: "How can we be happy again, now that our beloved person is gone? Does that mean we did not love them the way we believed we did?" In spite of these feelings—feelings expressed in the story about the reaction of some of the people to the loss of the Second Temple in Jerusalem in 70 CE—Jewish customs ask us to rise back to life. We "rise" from sitting shivah; we step back into the world; we slowly begin to take up our usual responsibilities. Which responsibilities do you feel ready for again? Which joys can you delight in again?
- Some of us might have difficulties eating while grieving; for others, food provides comfort and warmth. What has your relationship to food been since you lost your loved one? How, if at all, has it changed?

Poetry and Prayer

Soul Shine
Alden Solovy

Let your soul shine
In your chest.
Let your heart sparkle
In your eyes.
Let joy
Fill your limbs with radiance.
Let love

Fill your hands with splendor.
You are the instrument
Of God's music,
The tool
Of repairing the earth.
You are the voice
Of wonder and awe,
The song
Of hope and tomorrow.

This gift,
This majesty within,
Is not yours to keep.
It is not yours to hold.
It is not yours to hide.

Kaddish and Mourning Prayers

See page 175.

Week 6

Song

Ivdu et Adonai
Text: Psalm 100:2
Music: Moshe Shur

עִבְדוּ אֶת יְיָ בְּשִׂמְחָה, בֹּאוּ לְפָנָיו בִּרְנָנָה.
Ivdu et Adonai b'simchah, bo-u l'fanav birnanah.
Worship Adonai in gladness; come before God in song.

Kavanah

Sometimes, life is beautiful and we never want it to end. Other times, life is exhausting.

What do you think you will miss most about life when it is over?

Sacred Sources

We are heirs to a chaos of messianic dreams, piled up in the attic of our collective memory in no particular order at all. Jumbled together in a hopeless confusion, they defy us to sort them out. Will messiah come to a single generation? Why, then, should that generation be privileged above all others? And will that generation die or live right on into eternity? Where are the dead until messiah comes? In the Garden of Eden? Why, then, do they need redemption? And how about the resurrection? How will there be room for everybody in the world at the same time? And what about widows and widowers who remarry? Who will take care of all the fights? And how about transmigration? In which of its several bodies will the wandering soul appear? How about the glories of nature in messianic times? Will people really no longer have to plant in order to reap bounty? Will we live in this world or in the heavens? Is the messianic banquet a one-time event, or does it go on forever? Who will lead the *benschen*, and will they still sing it to that awful tune? And what happens afterward? After messiah, if there is an "after"? And after the resurrection? After the world is made perfect in God's kingdom? What happens *after* all that? (Arthur Green, *Seek My Face: A Jewish Mystical Theology*, p. 175)

- Most of the ideas about the afterlife listed by Arthur Green can be found in our prayer book. Read the questions he is raising carefully. Which of those ideas are you familiar with? Which ones are new to you? Which ones are relevant to you?
- To what an extent has the question of an afterlife been important to your grieving? Which ideas sound comforting to you? Which ones do you reject, and why?
- Some of us need certainty and proof in order to pray and believe; others choose to pray and believe in the face of uncertainty. What decision do you make? Why?

Poetry and Prayer

Afterlife
Chana Bloch

And then I rose
to the dazzle of light, to the pine trees
plunging and righting themselves in a furious wind.

To have died and come back again
raw, crackling,
and the numbness
stunned.

That clumsy
pushing and wheeling inside my chest, that ferocious
upturn—
I give myself to it. Why else
be in a body?

Something reaches inside me, finds the pocket
that sewed itself shut, turns it
precipitously
out into the air.

Kaddish and Mourning Prayers

See page 175.

Week 7

Song

Vaani t'filati
Text: Psalm 69:14
Music: Rabbi Josh Warshawsky and Yael Bettenhausen

וַאֲנִי תְפִלָּתִי לְךָ, יְיָ, עֵת רָצוֹן.
אֱלֹהִים, בְּרָב חַסְדֶּךָ, עֲנֵנִי בֶּאֱמֶת יִשְׁעֶךָ.

Vaani t'filati l'cha, Adonai, eit ratzon.
Elohim, b'rov chasdecha, aneini be-emet yishecha.

As for me, may my prayer come to You, Adonai, at a favorable time. O God, in Your abundant faithfulness, answer me with Your sure deliverance.

Kavanah

Sometimes we might want to focus on our private lives in order to take our minds off of difficult situations at work. Sometimes we flee into our work in order in order to escape our personal pain.

In what ways has your professional life, volunteering work, or a hobby been helpful to you in your mourning? When has it been a burden?

Sacred Sources

One suspends Torah study for the sake of burying the dead. (*Shulchan Aruch, Yoreh Dei-ah* 361:1)

As long as there is a dead person in town awaiting burial, all the townspeople are forbidden to engage in work. . . . However, if there are associations in town, each one of which attends to the burial needs of the dead on its particular day, it is permissible for the others who are not required to attend to the burial needs to engage in work. (*Shulchan Aruch, Yoreh Dei-ah* 343:1)

- Over the course of the last weeks and months, you have read many texts emphasizing the importance of burying the dead in Jewish tradition—and for close relatives, this obligation is not negotiable. However, there is no obligation to take care of the burial of people we do not know, as long as we make sure that everyone in our communities gets buried in dignity. Is this a given in your communities? When is it a given, and when not? Do you have ways to contribute to this issue?

- We are often asked to show empathy for mourners, even if we did not know the deceased. Has the experience of mourning enhanced your ability to understand others who go through a time of grief? What have you learned about grief?
- Over the last few weeks, people might have shown you different kinds of support, empathy, or simply a way to preserve the normalcy of daily life while your life was turned upside down. What kinds of behavior have been most helpful to you? How could you do something similar for someone else in mourning?

Poetry and Prayer

Dust

Dorianne Laux

Someone spoke to me last night,
told me the truth. Just a few words,
but I recognized it.
I knew I should make myself get up,
write it down, but it was late,
and I was exhausted from working
all day in the garden, moving rocks.
Now, I remember only the flavor—
not like food, sweet or sharp.
More like a fine powder, like dust.
And I wasn't elated or frightened,
but simply rapt, aware.
That's how it is sometimes—
God comes to your window,
all bright light and black wings,
and you're just too tired to open it.

Kaddish and Mourning Prayers

See page 175.

GRATITUDE

Living with Your Memory

Week 1

Song

Et'haleich Lifnei Yah
Text: Psalm 116:9
Music: Rabbi Shefa Gold

אֶתְהַלֵּךְ לִפְנֵי יָהּ בְּאַרְצוֹת הַחַיִּים.
Et'haleich lifnei Yah, b'artzot hachayim.
I will walk before God in the lands of the living
I will walk before God in the Lands of Life.

Kavanah

At times, grief might still rise within you like a mighty wave that can topple you over.

Do you have the power to hold that wave back if the moment is not right? How can memories of your beloved one help you to ground yourself and limit the pain of your current state of grief?

Sacred Sources

> I call heaven and earth to witness against you this day: I have put before you life and death, blessing and curse. Choose life—if you and your offspring would live—by loving the Eternal your God, heeding God's commands, and holding fast to [God]. (Deuteronomy 30:19–20)

> Life and death: comprise all that a person is "given"—all the facets of a person's character, his inborn traits and tendencies, his upbringing and environment; all those factors which determine what he calls "life," what presents itself to him as "good" and "true"; and equally what he calls "death," evil" and "falsehood." All these things "I have put before you," literally: "I have given before you; these are the "givens" of the human situation; they exist independently of any action on our part, like all the other features of our environment. But—"you shall choose life." "Choosing life," choosing truth and reality, is something which only the human being himself can do, and which he does without being affected

by any outside factor whatsoever. (Rabbi Eliyahu Dessler, *Michtav Me-Eliyahu,* first part trans. by Rabbi Aryeh Carmell as *Strive for Truth,* vol. 2, p. 56–57.)

- What do you call "life"? What presents itself to you as "good" and "true"—and as "evil" and "false"?
- How often do you have the sense that you are actively choosing one over the other? What can you do to increase the frequency of those active decisions?
- You may have noticed that many things are not "either good or evil," but contain a bit of both. How does this fact change your perception of what Eliyahu Dessler calls "life"?

Poetry and Prayer

By the Well of Living and Seeing: 36
Charles Reznikoff

The invitation read: not to mourn
but to rejoice in a good life.
The widower, his false teeth showing in a wide smile,
entered
and turning from side to side,
greeted us.
He began by reading a long essay on his dead wife.
And as he read, we heard those who were washing dishes in
the rear of the hotel's restaurant
joking and laughing about some matter of their own.
At the end, we were asked to stand
while the widower recited the ancient prayer of mourning—
used at first at all religious gatherings of Jews only to
glorify God—
and yet, even as he read,
he began to cry.

Kaddish and Mourning Prayers

See page 175.

Week 2

Song

Limnot Yameinu
Text: Psalm 90:12
Music: Rabbi Yitzhak Husbands-Hankin

לִמְנוֹת יָמֵינוּ כֵּן הוֹדַע וְנָבִא לְבַב חָכְמָה.

Limnot yameinu ken hoda v'navi l'vav chochmah.

Teach us to treasure our days, that we may open our hearts to Your wisdom.

Kavanah

In the midst of our day-to-day lives, we often lose sight of our simplest truths—we forget what we want our life to be about.

Close your eyes for a second and think about the Chasidic saying that one can learn Torah by watching a cat. What kind of Torah—what kind of "teaching"—would someone learn by watching you go about your life?

Sacred Sources

> Then God Eternal fashioned the man—dust from the soil—and breathed into his nostrils the breath of life, so that the man became a living being. (Genesis 2:7)

> A further word: Against them, my son, be warned!
> The making of many books is without limit
> And much study is a wearying of the flesh.
> The sum of the matter when all is said and done: Revere God and observe God's commandments! (Ecclesiastes 12:12–13)

- The story of Creation describes human life as a borrowed gift from God—a precious, temporal thing. Ecclesiastes asks us about the ultimate value of this gift: How are we supposed to use it, enjoy it, treat it? How can we thank God for it?
- Ecclesiastes also warns us of human pride and vanity. No matter how much we think we know, we will always be humbled

again by the power and mystery of life and death themselves. When in your life have you gone through an experience that corresponds to Ecclesiastes's warning?

- And yet, behind Ecclesiastes's seemingly gloomy words lies a deep and simple joyfulness. How would you describe the concept of a good life encompassed in Ecclesiastes's advice?

Poetry and Prayer

Mourner's Kaddish for Everyday

Debra Cash

Build me up of memory
loving and angry, tender and honest.
Let my loss build me a heart of wisdom,
compassion for the world's many losses.

Each hour is mortal
and each hour is eternal
and each hour is our testament.
May I create worthy memories
all the days of my life.

Kaddish and Mourning Prayers

See page 175.

Week 3

Song

We Are Loved
Text: Rabbi Rami Shapiro
Music: Shir Ya'akov Feit

We are embraced by arms that find us even when we are hidden from ourselves.
We are touched by fingers that soothe us even when we are too proud for soothing.
We are counseled by voices that guide us even when we are too embittered to hear.

We are loved by an unending love.

We are supported by hands that uplift us even in the midst of a fall.
We are urged on by eyes that meet us even when we are too weak for meeting.

We are loved by an unending love.

Embraced, touched, soothed, and counseled,
ours are the arms, the fingers, the voices;
ours are the hands, the eyes, the smiles;
We are loved by an unending love.

Kavanah

What is your life? A biological development? A gift from God? The product of all factors influencing you? A piece of art in your hands?

Sacred Sources

When the son of Rabbi Yochanan ben Zakkai (first century CE) died, his students came to console him. Rabbi Eliezer entered and sat before him and said, "Rabbi, do you wish me to say something to you?" He said to him, "Speak." He said to him, "Adam had a son and he died and he was consoled about his death. How do we know that he was consoled? As it is written, *Adam knew his wife again* [Genesis 4:25], so you too should be consoled." He said to him, "Is it not enough that I myself sorrow, that you mention Adam to me as well?" Rabbi Y'hoshua entered and said to him, "Rabbi, do you wish me to say something to you?" He said to him, "Speak." He said to him, "Job had sons and daughters and they all died on one day and he was consoled about them, so you too should be consoled. How do we know that in the case of Job? As it is written, *Adonai has given and Adonai has taken away, blessed be the name of Adonai* [Job 1:21]." He said to him, "Is it not enough that I myself sorrow, that you mention Job to me as well?" Rabbi Yosei entered and sat before him . . . he said to him, "Aaron had two great sons and they died on the same day, and he was consoled over their deaths, as it is written *Aaron was silent* [Leviticus 10:3]." Rabbi Shimon entered and said to him, "Rabbi do you wish . . . ?" . . . He said to him, "King David had a son and he died and he was consoled about his death, so you too should be consoled, as it is written, *David consoled his wife Bathsheba; he went to her and lay with her. She bore him a son and she named him Solomon* [II Samuel 12:24]." Rabbi Elazar ben Azariah entered and sat before him and said to him, "I will tell you a parable: To what is this similar? It is like a person with whom the king left a deposit for safekeeping. Every day he would cry and say, 'Woe is me, when will I be able to return this deposit safely?' So you too, Rabbi. You had a son who studied Torah, the Prophets, and the Writings, studied laws and *aggadot*, and died without sin. You should be consoled in that you returned your deposit whole." He said to him, "Rabbi Elazar, you have consoled me the [right] way that people console others." (*Avot D'Rabbi Natan* 14:6; English translation adapted from Shmuel Glick, *Light & Consolation*, pp. 73–74)

- *Avot D'Rabbi Natan* teaches that a much more important question than how we die is the question of how we live. What gives our lives meaning, according to the teaching of Elazar ben Azariah?
- What does "dying without sin" imply for you? Would you uphold "dying without sin" as a high value in life? Why or why not? Do you think the person you lost died "without sin"?
- The teaching from *Avot D'Rabbi Natan* emphasizes the

responsibility of parents for their children's ethical behavior. In fact, Jewish ethics speak of the concept of collective responsibility: each of us is responsible to step up when we see another "sinning." Have you, before you lost your beloved person, ever had to rebuke them? Do you remember them stepping up to you?

Poetry and Prayer

The Righteous
Martin Rawlings-Fein

We bless those luminaries of hope doing Your works without a thought of themselves, those motivated to make our world more ethical and equitable. Blessed are You, *Adonai* our God, for providing spiritual support and divine energy for those modern *tzadikim*.

Kaddish and Mourning Prayers

See page 175.

Week 4

Song

We Remember
Text: adapted from "We Remember Them"
by Rabbi Sylvan Kamens and Rabbi Jack Riemer
Music: Rabbi Ken Chasen and Rabbi Yoshi Zweiback

In the rising of the sun—we remember
In the blowing of the wind—we remember
In the opening of buds—we remember
We remember

In the blueness of the sky—we remember
In the rustling of the leaves—we remember
As the year starts and it ends—we remember
We remember

When we're weary and need strength—we remember
When we're lost and sick at heart—we remember
When we've joys we wish to share—we remember
We remember

So long as we live—they, too, shall live
They are now a part of us
They are now a part of us
They are now a part of us
As we remember
We remember
We remember

Kavanah

Well-meaning people seeking to comfort a mourner may say something like, "I hope you reach closure soon." However, complete closure is rarely attainable, and it may not even be desirable. Living with loss is not about closure. It is about learning to live with love and loss at the same time. It takes cultivating hope—not the hope that you will put death behind you, but that you will be able to carry the pain of your loss with you as you move forward.

Take a moment to reflect on this question: Where in your body do you carry the burden of your loss? Do you carry it in a place of growing strength and understanding? Do you carry it in a place of hardened muscles and growing exhaustion?

Sacred Sources

> The reality is that you will grieve forever. You will not "get over" the loss of a loved one; you will learn to live with it. You will heal, and you will rebuild yourself around the loss you have suffered. You will be whole again, but you will never be the same. Nor should you be the same, nor would you want to. (Elisabeth Kübler-Ross and David Kessler, *On Grief and Grieving*, p. 230)

- How does the assertion that you will grieve forever make you feel? Is this a truth you find easy to accept at this point? Why or why not?
- How does "rebuilding yourself" look for you? Which parts of your life and identity are you "rebuilding"? Do you have a sense of the new "whole" you—both the whole you as a complete person, and you as a healed person—that is evolving?
- If you could talk to your older self, the self before suffering this loss, what would you tell yourself? What do you know today that would have been helpful to know while stumbling into the "night-side" of life?

Poetry and Prayer

Cat in an Empty Apartment
Wisława Szymborska, translated from the Polish by Stanisław Barańczak and Clare Cavanagh

Die—you can't do that to a cat.
Since what can a cat do
in an empty apartment?
Climb the walls?
Rub up against the furniture?
Nothing seems different here

but nothing is the same.
Nothing's been moved
but there's more space.
And at nighttime no lamps are lit.

Footsteps on the staircase,
but they're new ones.
The hand that puts fish on the saucer
has changed, too.

Something doesn't start
at its usual time.
Something doesn't happen
as it should.
Someone was always, always here,
then suddenly disappeared
and stubbornly stays disappeared.

Every closet's been examined.
Every shelf has been explored.
Excavations under the carpet turned up nothing.
A commandment was even broken:
papers scattered everywhere.
What remains to be done.
Just sleep and wait.

Just wait till he turns up,
just let him show his face.
Will he ever get a lesson
on what not to do to a cat.
Sidle toward him
as if unwilling
and ever so slow
on visibly offended paws,
and no leaps or squeals at least to start.

Kaddish and Mourning Prayers

See page 175.

Week 5

Song

We Are Loved
Text: Rabbi Rami Shapiro
Music: Shir Ya'akov Feit

We are embraced by arms that find us even when we are hidden from ourselves.
We are touched by fingers that soothe us even when we are too proud for soothing.
We are counseled by voices that guide us even when we are too embittered to hear.

We are loved by an unending love.

We are supported by hands that uplift us even in the midst of a fall.
We are urged on by eyes that meet us even when we are too weak for meeting.

We are loved by an unending love.

Embraced, touched, soothed, and counseled,
ours are the arms, the fingers, the voices;
ours are the hands, the eyes, the smiles;
We are loved by an unending love.

Kavanah

Often, it is only our knowledge of the fragility of our bodies that keeps us from certain unhealthy behaviors.

How is this knowledge impacting your own behavior? What in your life explicitly serves the goal of prolonging or improving your life?

Sacred Sources

All living creatures are fated to die, but only human beings know it. Animals will instinctively protect themselves against threats to their life and well-being, but only human beings live in the valley of the shadow of death, with the knowledge that they are mortal, even when no one is attacking them. This knowledge that we are going to die someday changes our lives in many ways. It moves us to try to cheat death by doing something that will outlive us—having children, writing a book, having an impact on our friends and neighbors so that they will remember us fondly. Knowing that our time is limited gives value to the things we do. (Harold S. Kushner, *When Bad Things Happen to Good People*, p. 87)

- We humans are not necessarily aware of our mortality at any given hour. It is often the experience of losing someone we love that teaches us this painful lesson. In what ways has losing your loved one made you appreciate life more? When did it do the opposite?
- "Cheating death" by creating something that outlives us—do you think this is the core motivation to have children, write books, and seek to have an impact? What could be other motivations to pursue any one of those goals?
- How do you "cheat death"?

Poetry and Prayer

Angels Without Wings

Jane Vonnegut Yarmolinksy

Written while she was battling terminal cancer, Angels Without Wings *chronicles Yarmolinsky's experience bringing four orphaned nephews into her home and looks back on her marriage, which ended in divorce.*

So what is there to say when you know you don't have much time left? Or rather, what is most important to say, since you can't say it all? I wrote this partly to find out what I might have to say. In the doing I have discovered how absolutely madly in love I am with life and with all the people I was given—yes, given—to love. I am grateful to have learned so much of life: of the steadiness of personalities, the constancy of love, the preciousness of the moment, the fragility of time, the power of the imagination, the strength of that vital life force that enables us to hold each other up when our wings get broken. And perhaps, above all, I've learned that pain and joy are inextricably mingled and that out of suffering does come love. It is a great mystery to me why this should be so.

But I know that there will be angels in the next underpass as well, and I am content.

Kaddish and Mourning Prayers

See page 175.

Week 6

Song

Limnot Yameinu
Text: Psalm 90:12
Music: Rabbi Yitzhak Husbands-Hankin

לִמְנוֹת יָמֵינוּ כֵּן הוֹדַע וְנָבִא לְבַב חָכְמָה.
Limnot yameinu ken hoda v'navi l'vav chochmah.
Teach us to treasure our days, that we may open our hearts to Your wisdom.

Kavanah

There is a Jewish custom of writing an "ethical will" designed to pass down ethical values from one generation to the next.

What are some of the ethical teachings you learned from your loved one?

Sacred Sources

Toward the end of the Book of Deuteronomy, God tells Moses that he is about to die and invites him to come into the Tent of Meeting with Joshua, his successor, for some final counsel. God says that after Moses dies, Israel will abandon the covenant, and as a result, God will withdraw from them, and evil will befall them. God doesn't say this can be prevented; instead, God tells Moses to "write down this poem and teach it to the people" (Deuteronomy 31:19), so that they may remember their covenant with God.

The Eternal One said to Moses: The time is drawing near for you to die. Call Joshua and present yourselves in the Tent of Meeting that I may instruct him. Moses and Joshua went and presented themselves in the Tent of Meeting. The Eternal appeared in the Tent, in a pillar of cloud, the pillar of cloud having come to rest at the entrance of the tent.

The Eternal said to Moses: You are soon to lie with your ancestors. This people will thereupon go astray after the alien gods in their midst, in the land that they are about to enter; they will forsake Me and break My covenant that I made with them. Then My anger will flare up against them, and I will abandon them and hide My countenance from them. They shall be ready prey; and many evils and troubles shall befall them. And they shall say on that day, "Surely it is because our God is not in our midst that these evils have befallen us." Yet I will keep My countenance hidden on that day, because of all the evil they have done in turning to other gods. Therefore, write down this poem and teach it to the people of Israel; put it in their mouths, in order that this poem may be My witness against the people of Israel. (Deuteronomy 31:14–19)

- What purpose is behind God's instruction to Moses and Joshua to "write down this poem and teach it to the people"?
- How might you understand your relationship with the person you are mourning in terms of a covenant? What were some of the terms that made this relationship so special?
- How might remembering this covenant help you move forward?

Poetry and Prayer

Just Beyond Yourself
David Whyte

Just beyond
yourself.
It's where
you need
to be.
Half a step
into
self-forgetting
and the rest
restored
by what
you'll meet.
There is a road
always beckoning.
When you see
the two sides

of it
closing together
at that far horizon
and deep in
the foundations
of your own
heart
at exactly
the same
time,
that's how
you know
it's the road
you
have
to follow.
That's how
you know
it's where
you
have
to go.
That's how
you know
you have
to go.
That's
how you know.
Just beyond
yourself,
it's
where you
need to be.

Kaddish and Mourning Prayers

See page 175.

Week 7

Song

Gesher (The Whole World Is a Narrow Bridge)
Text: Rabbi Nachman of Bratzlav
Music: Rabbi Yosef Goldman

Kol haolam kulo, gesher tzar m'od,
gesher tzar m'od, gesher tzar m'od.
Kol haolam kulo, gesher tzar m'od,
gesher tzar m'od.
V'ha-ikar, v'ha-ikar lo l'facheid,
lo l'facheid k'lal.
V'ha-ikar, v'ha-ikar lo l'facheid,
lo l'facheid k'lal.

כָּל הָעוֹלָם כֻּלּוֹ, גֶּשֶׁר צַר מְאֹד,
גֶּשֶׁר צַר מְאֹד, גֶּשֶׁר צַר מְאֹד.
כָּל הָעוֹלָם כֻּלּוֹ, גֶּשֶׁר צַר מְאֹד,
גֶּשֶׁר צַר מְאֹד.
וְהָעִיקָר, וְהָעִיקָר לֹא לְפַחֵד,
לֹא לְפַחֵד כְּלָל.
וְהָעִיקָר, וְהָעִיקָר לֹא לְפַחֵד,
לֹא לְפַחֵד כְּלָל.

All the world is a narrow bridge, and the main rule is not to be afraid at all. (*Likutei Moharan*, Part II 48:2)

Kavanah

The death of a loved one is almost always a profoundly disruptive event filled with deep loss and pain. Indeed, we may never achieve "closure" after such a death, and there is no reason to think that this should be the goal. Yet, we do go on living, and the dead live within us.

In what way, if any, can you relate Rabbi Nachman's "narrow bridge" to the journey of mourning you are on?

Sacred Sources

If any of you are around when I have to meet my day, I don't want a long funeral. And if you get somebody to deliver the eulogy, tell them not to talk too long. And every now and then I wonder what I want them to say. Tell them not to mention that I have a Nobel Peace Prize—that isn't important. Tell them not to mention that I have three or four hundred other awards—that's not important. Tell them not to mention where I went to school.

I'd like somebody to mention that day that Martin Luther King, Jr., tried to give his life serving others. I'd like for somebody to say that day that Martin Luther King, Jr., tried to love somebody. I want you to say that day that I tried to be right on the war question. I want you to be able to say that day that I did try to feed the hungry. And I want you to be able to say that day that I did try in my life to clothe those who were naked. I want you to say on that day that I did try in my life to visit those who were in prison. I want you to say that I tried to love and serve humanity.

Yes, if you want to say that I was a drum major, say that I was a drum major for justice. Say that I was a drum major for peace. I was a drum major for righteousness. And all of the other shallow things will not matter. I won't have any money to leave behind. I won't have the fine and luxurious things of life to leave behind. But I just want to leave a committed life behind. And that's all I want to say.

If I can help somebody as I pass along,
If I can cheer somebody with a word or song,
If I can show somebody he's traveling wrong,
Then my living will not be in vain.

(Excerpt from the last sermon delivered by the
Reverend Dr. Martin Luther King at the Ebenezer
Baptist Church in Atlanta, Georgia, February 4, 1968)

- Which of his achievements does Dr. King seem to be most proud of? What values are expressed by his preferences?
- How might the person you lost have wished to be remembered? What do you think they would have wanted to be their legacy?
- Today, or at some point this week, think of something you can do to honor this legacy. When you are done, take a moment to remember the soul of your loved one, and think about something you would like to tell them.

Poetry and Prayer

Do Not Stand at My Grave and Weep

Mary Elizabeth Frye

Do not stand at my grave and weep,
I am not there, I do not sleep.
I am in a thousand winds that blow,

I am the softly falling snow.
I am the gentle showers of rain,
I am the fields of ripening grain.
I am in the morning hush,
I am in the graceful rush
Of beautiful birds in circling flight,
I am the starshine of the night.
I am in the flowers that bloom,
I am in a quiet room.
I am in the birds that sing,
I am in each lovely thing.
Do not stand at my grave and cry,
I am not there. I do not die.

Kaddish and Mourning Prayers

See page 175.

GROUP RITUALS

A Ritual for after the Funeral: Beginning to Sit Shivah

A Ritual to Mark the End of Shivah

A Ritual to Mark the End of *Sh'loshim*

Matzeivah (Unveiling of the Tombstone): A Ritual for Revisiting

Marking the *Yahrzeit*: A Ritual of Transitioning

A Ritual for after the Funeral: Beginning to Sit Shivah

RETURNING HOME after the funeral of a loved one may be one of life's most disorienting experiences. After a death, the experience of loss often makes us turn inward. Many find that they do not have enough inner resources to face the time that lies ahead of them, and they look for sources of wisdom, support, comfort, and guidance. Jewish community and Jewish learning can be powerful sources of such support.

Jewish tradition includes a variety of practices that acknowledge the profound disruption that occurs with a death. Among them is the ritual of sitting shivah. The word *shivah* means "seven," and the traditional practice is to sit for seven days, starting on the day of burial and ending on the morning of the seventh day. During this time, much of normal life is upended. Mourners refrain from work, from wearing leather shoes, from engaging in sexual activity, from studying Torah, and some even from bathing. A practice shared by many other religious communities includes covering all the mirrors in the home as a way of discouraging excessive grooming or adornment; a more mystical interpretation suggests that covering the mirrors may prevent the reflection of evil spirits or inner demons that may rise up during this time of deep grief.

When mourners return home after the funeral, the traditional practice is to eat a meal of consolation. For many, eating may feel like the last thing they want to do in this moment—but at the same time, eating something might be a good way to hold on to life, even if life will never be the same. It is a custom to include round foods in this meal, symbolizing the circle of life and renewal. Lentils, bagels, olives . . . anything round will do!

Today, many people shorten the period of shivah to three days or even less. Jewish tradition acknowledges the challenges of taking off such a lengthy period of time and allows those who must to return to work after three days. For a wide variety of reasons, some shorten shivah even more.

Typically, specific hours are set for visitors to come visit during the period of shivah, however long it lasts. Often, the greatest number of people come during the times set aside for prayer, which give the mourner the opportunity to recite the Mourner's *Kaddish* with a minyan, a "quorum of ten." Visitors often bring food and provide help to set up and clean up so that the mourners can devote their emotional and spiritual attention to absorbing their new reality. One practice that some find difficult to follow is to refrain from conversation until the mourner speaks to them. What mourners most often need from their visitors is a safe space to sit quietly, share their stories, and find solace in the comfort of others.

For mourners: Share with your visitors how friendships and connections to family members may help you most during this time of mourning.

Song

Hinei Mah Tov
Text: Psalm 133:1
Music: Sufi

הִנֵּה מַה טּוֹב וּמַה נָּעִים שֶׁבֶת אַחִים גַּם יָחַד.
Hineih mah tov umah na-im shevet achim gam yachad.
How good and pleasant it is for us to sit together as kin.

Sacred Sources

Traditionally, the Kaddish *is understood to be the obligation of a mourner who is marking the death of a close relative like a parent, sibling, spouse, or child. The* Kaddish *is not a biblical prayer, but the custom of reciting it aloud is deeply embedded in Jewish practice.*

The origins of the prayer date to the Second Temple period (destroyed in 70 CE). It began as a prayer for the end of study sessions and then was gradually introduced into the synagogue service (Babylonian Talmud, Sotah *49a; Lawrence A. Hoffman, ed.,* Traditional Prayers, Modern Commentaries, *vol. 6, p. 160). The association of the* Kaddish *with mourners was solidified between the twelfth and thirteenth centuries, during the period of the Crusades in Europe. A variety of sources suggest that many of the survivors believed that reciting the* Kaddish *would shorten the amount of time the deceased would spend in Gehenna before ascending to heaven (Diamant,* Saying Kaddish: How to Comfort the Dying, Bury the Dead, and Mourn as a Jew*). One example of this is a tale attributed to Rabbi Akiva, "who came across a man suffering terrible torments in hell. The rabbi found the poor man's long-lost son and taught him to recite the verse 'May [God's] great name be blessed.' With those words, the father's soul was released and rose up to heaven" (Diamant,* Saying Kaddish, *p. 28; based on a midrash from* Seder Eliyahu Zuta).

- How do you relate to the idea that reciting the *Kaddish* helps the soul of the deceased to "rise up to heaven"?
- Who is the *Kaddish* for?

Over time, the custom developed for a man (and, more recently, any adult) to say Kaddish *every day for a year for a deceased parent. Some people recite* Kaddish *for a full twelve months, while others stop at eleven months because of a midrash (Babylonian Talmud,* Sanhedrin *104a) that says that even the most wicked people are consigned to hell for a maximum of twelve months. No one wants to think of a parent as "most wicked," so the tradition of saying* Kaddish *for only eleven months evolved. Saying* Kaddish *for loved ones other than a parent is mandated only for the first thirty days, but many continue reciting the prayer for a full year.*

In halachic communities, Kaddish *is recited only if at least a minyan of ten adults (men) is present. Some communities, because of their small size or for other reasons, do not require a full quorum of ten for* Kaddish *to be said. There is historical precedent for this practice. In the early Middle Ages, the definition of a minyan was not yet very rigid. In* Tractate Sof'rim *10:8, we read that a minyan is required for the recitation of certain prayers, but it is added: "Our sages in Palestine recite these prayers in the presence of seven . . . and some say even in the presence of only six" (Abraham Millgram,* Jewish Worship, *p. 343). The Palestinian practice was overruled, and the Babylonian custom of requiring a minyan of ten became the normative practice for Jews everywhere. However, in recognition of the mourning process as a personal journey, some liberal communities in recent times have lifted the ten-person restriction and invite people to recite* Kaddish *as they feel the need.*

> One does not recite the introductory prayers and blessings before the *Sh'ma*; nor does one pass before the ark to repeat the *Amidah*, nor do the priests lift their hands to recite the Priestly Blessing, nor is the Torah read in public, nor does one conclude with a read-

ing from the Prophets in the presence of fewer than ten. And one does not observe the practice of standing up and sitting down for the delivery of eulogies at a funeral service; nor does one recite the mourners' blessing or comfort mourners in two lines after the funeral; or recite the bridegrooms' blessing; and one does not invite others to recite Grace after Meals, with the name of God, with fewer than ten present. (Mishnah, *M'gillah* 4:3)

- Why do you think the Rabbis decided to institute the requirement of a minyan?
- If you recite *Kaddish*, when and how do you say it in community?
- In what ways, if any, do you mourn in community?

Poetry and Prayer

Seven Stops
Rabbi Rachel Barenblat

The Zohar says
after death
each soul is judged
seven times.

Pallbearers make
seven stops
on the way
to the grave

which means
our progress
shambles, pauses
begins again

as though
we were reluctant
to reach
that destination.

Seven: the days
of the week
the colors

of the rainbow
seven weeks
of the Omer
between Pesach planting
and Shavuot harvest.

For what
will you be judged
when your journey
has ended?

Kaddish and Mourning Prayers

See page 175.

A Ritual to Mark the End of Shivah

Adapted, with permission, from a ritual by
Rabbi Lawrence Hoffman, PhD

FOR MANY JEWS, sitting shivah ends on the morning of the seventh day. Today, some shorten their shivah to three days or even fewer. Regardless of the number of its days, the beginning of the shivah is usually recognized communally; but it probably ends without any communal notice at all, even though the end of the shivah seems to be an important moment in the journey of mourning. Most mourners are at a loss for what to do—except, perhaps, to go for a walk around the block.

The following ritual builds on informal practices of the past. It should take place *whenever the last communal gathering occurs*. If, for example, mourners observe three days of shivah, including one hour only on the third morning, the ritual would occur the evening of the day prior. Frequently, families begin shivah together but end it separately. When a parent dies, for instance, children may begin shivah together in their deceased parent's home but then disperse to conclude their mourning with their own community. In such cases, they may keep just a single night of shivah in their own home, in which case the following ritual might well serve as a particularly important closing of the evening, a way to mark the local shivah gathering in a spiritually fulfilling manner.

In our age, mourners may choose to convene as a virtual community to mark the end of shivah. All that is needed is someone to play the role of ritual *facilitator*. The facilitator should be a person close to the mourners, but it should not be one of the mourners themselves. This ritual is a gift to them, to ease the transition back into the world outside of their homes. The mourners should be seated on a sofa (or low chair or stool) and, if need be, on extra chairs arranged as extensions of the sofa, on either side of it. They should all be facing the computer camera, able to speak together as they read their part. They will be asked, at the end, to hold hands and rise together.

If the ritual occurs in the context of a shivah minyan, it should be inserted into the service just prior to *Aleinu*. If not, it can occur at any opportune moment, preferably when the largest number of people are in attendance, either in person or online. Shivah actually ends the next morning, but mourners may have no one present at that time.

Prepare the following ritual objects:

- A wine cup, filled with wine or grape juice, the kind normally used for *Kiddush* on Shabbat.
- The large shivah candle from the funeral home or another lit candle, if available, which should be placed beside the wine cup.
- The following prayer written out in large-enough script for all the mourners to read together or on separate note-cards that mourners individually may hold at the time of the reading.

Prayer

The prophet Isaiah proclaimed: "Your sun shall set no more. Your moon no more withdraw. For the Eternal shall be a light to you forever; and your days of mourning shall be ended" (Isaiah 60:20).

O God, who fills the emptiness of Your people's hearts, fill the emptiness that we now feel within ourselves, that we may know life and peace. Show us kindness and grace, goodness and love, that our lives be not lacking in all that is good.

בָּרוּךְ אַתָּה, יְיָ, מְנַחֵם לֵב אֲבֵלִים.

Baruch atah, Adonai, m'nacheim lev aveilim.

Blessed is God, who brings comfort
to the hearts of mourners.

Song

HaMakom Y'nacheim

Text: Tradition

Music: Rabbi Hanna Tiferet Siegel

הַמָּקוֹם יְנַחֵם אֶתְכֶם בְּתוֹךְ שְׁאַר אֲבֵלֵי צִיּוֹן וִירוּשָׁלָיִם.

HaMakom y'nacheim et-chem b'toch sh'ar aveilei Tziyon virushalayim.

May God comfort you, together with the mourners
of Zion and Jerusalem.

Ritual

FACILITATOR READS:

In times past, our ancestors would pour a cup of wine for those in mourning. It was called *kos tanchumin*, "the cup of consolation." As a gesture of love and support, their family and friends would gather in their homes as we do now with you. The mourners would drink the wine as a symbol of their faith in God's presence, even at the worst of times—a faith made possible, perhaps, because of the friends and family who were present to them, their community, through whom it became evident that somehow, someday, God would heal them of their grief.

Look, then, at the faces of those who stand by you now, the people present to you, in person or on camera. Your shivah ends tomorrow morning after a single hour, at which time you are free to undertake your normal responsibilities. If you are able, take a walk outside your home, a symbolic set of steps to symbolize the act of returning to the world of work and regularity. Tonight, however, the last night of shivah, we, your friends and extended family, ask you to taste from the cup of consolation and then read a prayer of hope, that you may hear us say "Amen," our conviction that God will be with you, as, indeed, we will be as well, to help you in the inevitable moments of emptiness that you will feel even after shivah has long become a thing of memory.

FACILITATOR RECITES the following blessing over wine; mourners may wish to say it along with the facilitator:

בָּרוּךְ אַתָּה, יְיָ אֱלֹהֵינוּ, מֶלֶךְ הָעוֹלָם, בּוֹרֵא פְּרִי הַגָּפֶן.

Baruch atah, Adonai Eloheinu, Melech haolam, borei p'ri hagafen.

Blessed are You, Adonai our God, Creator of the fruit of the vine.

FACILITATOR:

"To which we all say, "Amen."

We ask, as well, that you now read aloud, together, the ancient prayer of our people, the Prayer of Consolation, the request for God's kindness, grace, and goodness.

MOURNERS pick up the prayer written on their sheets of paper and read it together: "The prophet Isaiah proclaimed..." (see text above)

FACILITATOR:

To which we all say, from near and far away, "Amen."

Just days ago, you held one another in preparation for the funeral. I ask you once again to hold each other close, holding hands with one another and, virtually, with all of us, who reach out to you from afar, to hold you in virtual embrace. Know that just as God will be with you in the days and weeks and months that follow, so too will we.

I ask you, while still holding hands, to pull each other up from shivah . . . and as you do so, feel the strength in one another's grasp.

Holding hands, the MOURNERS pull one another up, off the sofa and chairs on which they have been sitting. As they do so, they naturally tighten their grasp of one another, feeling the strength that binds them together.

FACILITATOR:

We pray that when your shivah ends tomorrow morning, you will recall that strength and know that even from afar, we all hold hands with you. May you go *michayil ad chayil*, "from strength to strength." To which we all say, "Amen."

Rising

In eighteenth-century Germany it was customary for the entire Book of Psalms to be recited in the mourners' home during the week of shivah, so that the completion of the final psalm would signal the end of the mourning period. Try reading a psalm each day, and plan to rise up from your shivah with Psalm 150.

Poetry and Prayer

Kaddish*: You Ask So Much*

Rabbi Karyn D. Kedar

To the God of the bereaved.

Yitkadash.
May the sacred become
the vessel for my suffering.
Amen.

May I declare Your greatness
v'yitgadal and dwell in grandeur and
devotion, now, and forever.
Amen.

May I find comfort in this moment
of immense loss. *Sh'mei Raba.*
Your name is Great Abundance.
Amen.

Help me, O God of the mourner.
Comfort me.

May my grief open my heart
to compassion and understanding.
Amen.

This.
Only this.

Amen and amen.

Kaddish and Mourning Prayers

See page 175.

A Ritual to Mark the End of Sh'loshim

THE FOLLOWING RITUAL is envisioned as a home-based ritual for three to fifteen people. The ritual can be done in an hour, but you can also take your time and spend a couple of hours together—talking, reading, singing, sharing memories, eating, and simply being there for each other.

Thirty days after the death of a dear one, we are facing major transitions in our own life. We may be past the initial feelings of shock and brokenness, but we are still close to death, close to memories, close to unfinished business, and close to the pain over all the moments that will no longer be shared.

Invite your guests to share brief stories about a happy memory of the deceased. Ask them to prepare in advance.

Song

Each of Us Has a Name
Text: Zelda, translated by Marcia Lee Falk
Music: Hanan Yuval and Chava Alberstein

לְכָל אִישׁ יֵשׁ שֵׁם
שֶׁנָּתַן לוֹ אֱלֹהִים וְנָתְנוּ לוֹ אָבִיו וְאִמּוֹ.

לְכָל אִישׁ יֵשׁ שֵׁם
שֶׁנָּתְנוּ לוֹ קוֹמָתוֹ וְאֹפֶן חִיּוּכוֹ וְנָתַן לוֹ הָאָרִיג.

לְכָל אִישׁ יֵשׁ שֵׁם
שֶׁנָּתְנוּ לוֹ הֶהָרִים וְנָתְנוּ לוֹ כְּתָלָיו.

לְכָל אִישׁ יֵשׁ שֵׁם
שֶׁנָּתְנוּ לוֹ הַמַּזָּלוֹת וְנָתְנוּ לוֹ שְׁכֵנָיו.

לְכָל אִישׁ יֵשׁ שֵׁם
שֶׁנָּתְנוּ לוֹ חֲטָאָיו וְנָתְנָה לוֹ כְּמִיהָתוֹ.

לְכָל אִישׁ יֵשׁ שֵׁם
שֶׁנָּתְנוּ לוֹ שׂוֹנְאָיו וְנָתְנָה לוֹ אַהֲבָתוֹ.

לְכָל אִישׁ יֵשׁ שֵׁם
שֶׁנָּתְנוּ לוֹ חַגָּיו וְנָתְנָה לוֹ מְלָאכְתּוֹ.

לְכָל אִישׁ יֵשׁ שֵׁם
שֶׁנָּתְנוּ לוֹ תְּקוּפוֹת הַשָּׁנָה וְנָתַן לוֹ עִוְרוֹנוֹ.

לְכָל אִישׁ יֵשׁ שֵׁם
שֶׁנָּתַן לוֹ הַיָּם וְנָתַן לוֹ מוֹתוֹ.

Each of us has a name
given by God
and given by our parents.

Each of us has a name
given by our stature and our smile
and given by what we wear.

Each of us has a name
given by the mountains
and given by our walls.

Each of us has a name
given by the stars
and given by our neighbors.

Each of us has a name
given by our sins
and given by our longing.

Each of us has a name
given by our enemies
and given by our love.

Each of us has a name
given by our celebrations
and given by our work.

Each of us has a name
given by the seasons
and given by our blindness.

Each of us has a name
given by the sea
and given by
our death.

Sacred Sources

The Book of Ecclesiastes addresses one of the main questions of life: How do we live lives of meaning, purpose, and pleasure even when we know it is all *hevel*: "ephemeral, absurd, incomprehensible, and perhaps even futile"?

> A season is set for everything, a time for every experience
> under heaven:
> A time for being born and a time for dying;
> A time for planting and a time for uprooting the planted;
> A time for slaying and a time for healing;
> A time for tearing down and a time for building up;
> A time for weeping and a time for laughing;
> A time for wailing and a time for dancing;
> A time for throwing stones and a time for gathering stones;
> A time for embracing and a time for shunning embraces;
> A time for seeking and a time for discarding;
> A time for ripping and a time for sewing;
> A time for silence and a time for speaking;
> A time for loving and a time for hating;
> A time for war and a time for peace.
> What value, then, can we, the people of affairs, get from
> what we earn?
> (Ecclesiastes 3:1–9)

- What do you think is the main message of this poem?
- What effect does the pairing of opposites have on you?
- The word *eit*, translated as "time," is repeated throughout the poem. In the JPS commentary on *Kohelet*, Michael V. Fox writes, "'Time' here is not a specific moment in time but

rather an occasion or situation that is right for something.... This does not imply that the moments when we fight or laugh are predetermined and independent of human decision, but rather certain occasions demand a certain type of response." (Michael V. Fox, *The JPS Bible Commentary: Ecclesiastes*, p.20) What feels "right" at this moment?

Poetry and Prayer

When Will I Be Myself Again
Rabbi Lewis John Eron

"When will I be myself again?"
Some Tuesday, perhaps,
In the late afternoon,
Sitting quietly with a cup of tea,
And a cookie;
Or Wednesday, same time or later,
You will stir from a nap and see her;
You will pick up the phone to call her;
You will hear her voice—unexpected advice—
And maybe argue.
And you will not be frightened,
And you will not be sad,
And you will not be alone,
Not alone at all,
And your tears will warm you.
But not today,
And not tomorrow,
And not tomorrow's tomorrow,
But some day,
Some Tuesday, late in the afternoon,
Sitting quietly with a cup of tea,
And a cookie;
And you will be yourself again.

Kaddish and Mourning Prayers

See page 175.

Matzeivah (*Unveiling of the Tombstone*): *A Ritual for Revisiting*

THERE IS NO SET LITURGY associated with unveiling the gravestone. Traditions differ based on the community and the desires and needs of family members and friends. The gathering takes place at the graveside and may include the reading of psalms and prayers, as well as sharing of stories and appreciations. One common tradition is to place a stone on the marker, as a sign of love and enduring memory—a symbolic way of lifting the weight of the stone off our hearts and taking a step back into life.

In Israel, the unveiling often takes place at the end of *sh'loshim*, the first thirty days after the death. In the United States, many families wait until the end of the first six months, and sometimes even longer, to gather and mark this passage.

Whenever you choose to set the grave marker in place, take the time to reflect on something you have learned about your relationship to your loved one over this period of mourning.

Share a brief story.

Invite others to share their comforting memories, too.

Song

Yosheiv B'seiter Elyon
Text: Psalm 91:4–5, 12
Music: Norma Brooks

בְּאֶבְרָתוֹ יָסֶךְ לָךְ וְתַחַת כְּנָפָיו תֶּחְסֶה צִנָּה וְסֹחֵרָה אֲמִתּוֹ.
לֹא תִירָא מִפַּחַד לָיְלָה מֵחֵץ יָעוּף יוֹמָם . . . .
עַל כַּפַּיִם יִשָּׂאוּנְךָ פֶּן תִּגֹּף בָּאֶבֶן רַגְלֶךָ.

B'evrato yasech lach v'tachat k'nafav techseh tzinah v'socheirah amito.
Lo tira mipachad lailah meicheitz ya-uf yomam. . . .
Al kapayim yisa-uncha pen tigof ba-even raglecha.

With pinions God will protect you, under God's wings you will find refuge, with God's faithfulness a shield and a wall.

You shall not fear from the terror of night, from the arrow let fly by day. . . .
[The angels] will lift you up in their hands, lest your foot strike a rock.

Sacred Sources

Rabbi Zoë Klein

It is customary for Jews to place a stone
by the graveside of one they respect and love.
Some say that this is just a marker
to commemorate the visit.
Some say
that it is to weigh down the spirits of grief that haunt us,
anchoring our pain
so that we do not dismiss our destiny
and walk the path of a mourner forever.

I like to believe that the stone
has more to do with "foundation,"
the first brick,
laid in building a future
that at one time seemed inconceivable;
a future where ________ [my loved one]
is not at the table—
at our side, a phone call away—
a world without their radiance.

That future once seemed inconceivable
but here we are,
and these stones say:
today we begin to build a new future
a future where our spirits
are clothed in love,
our hearts are branded with goodness,
a future in which ________ is woven into us,
wrapped around us,
lighting our way,

where we know that every joy we encounter
is celebrated from on high as well.

- What qualities of the person whose grave is being unveiled are now part of you?
- What haunts you?
- What makes you feel the presence of your lost loved one in your life?

Poetry and Prayer

El Malei Rachamim (God, Full of Compassion)

El malei rachamim, shochein bamromim. Hamtzei m'nuchah n'chonah tachat kanfei hash'chinah, im k'doshim ut'horim, k'zohar harakia mazhirim, l'nishmot yakireinu shehalchu l'olamam. Baal harachamim, yastireim b'seiter k'nafav l'olamim. V'yitzror bitzror hachayim et nishmatam. Adonai hu nachalatam, v'yanuchu b'shalom al mishkavam. V'nomar: Amen.	אֵל מָלֵא רַחֲמִים, שׁוֹכֵן בַּמְּרוֹמִים. הַמְצֵא מְנוּחָה נְכוֹנָה תַּחַת כַּנְפֵי הַשְּׁכִינָה, עִם קְדוֹשִׁים וּטְהוֹרִים, כְּזֹהַר הָרָקִיעַ מַזְהִירִים, לְנִשְׁמוֹת יַקִּירֵינוּ שֶׁהָלְכוּ לְעוֹלָמָם. בַּעַל הָרַחֲמִים, יַסְתִּירֵם בְּסֵתֶר כְּנָפָיו לְעוֹלָמִים. וְיִצְרוֹר בִּצְרוֹר הַחַיִּים אֶת נִשְׁמָתָם. יְיָ הוּא נַחֲלָתָם, וְיָנוּחוּ בְּשָׁלוֹם עַל מִשְׁכָּבָם. וְנֹאמַר: אָמֵן.

O God, full of compassion—*El Malei Rachamim*, please send Your comfort to those who grieve. Help them to dispel the sadness that accompanies the pain of loss, and to find joy in the precious memories of ________. May Your love inspire them to focus on the love they have for ________, and that ________ had for them.

Help them to face the future with courage, to treasure their loved one's legacy. Sustain us in our faith, O God, even in this troubling time, as You have sustained us in times of trouble and sorrow throughout the generations.

Blessed are You, Adonai, who provides comfort to the broken-hearted.

Kaddish and Mourning Prayers

See page 175.

Marking the Yahrzeit: A Ritual of Transitioning

Sorrow comes in great waves. . . . But it rolls over us, and though it may almost smother us it leaves us on the spot, and we know that if it is strong we are stronger, inasmuch as it passes and we remain. It wears us, uses us, but we wear it and use it in return; and it is blind, whereas, we after a manner see . . . everything will pass, and serenity and accepted mysteries and disillusionments, and the tenderness of a few good people, and new opportunities and ever so much of life, in a word, will remain. —*Henry James*

THERE IS NO SET pattern to mourning the death of someone we love. It can come upon us suddenly, or it can linger over a long stretch of time, changing in tone and texture as we go about our daily lives. We know that mourning can last far longer than a single year. We also know that the first year is almost always the most difficult. Every month that goes by is a month farther from the loved one we lost. Holidays and personal milestones become sites of memory for what happened a year ago at the same season, in happier times.

For some people, things begin to change at the end of the first year. As the routines and demands of living resume some sense of normalcy, longer stretches of time may go by before the loss reenters consciousness—and then it is there again. Grief ebbs and flows.

The end of the first year is often a good time for reflection. For mourners, this may be time to gather a close circle of family or friends. If the timing fits, this gathering could occur around Yom Kippur or one of the three major Jewish festivals—Passover, Shavuot, or Sukkot. These are the set times for when the memorial service, *Yizkor*, is traditionally recited in community. Whether one goes to synagogue or not, convening a personal *Yizkor* ritual provides an opportunity to sing and study, share stories, and pray together as a way of giving an extra measure of honor to the loved one who has died.

Share a memory of your loved one that brings you joy.

Song

We Can Rise
Text: Psalm 121:1–2
English Text and Music: Chana Rothman

אֶשָּׂא עֵינַי אֶל־הֶהָרִים מֵאַיִן יָבֹא עֶזְרִי
עֶזְרִי מֵעִם יְיָ, עֹשֵׂה שָׁמַיִם וָאָרֶץ.

CHORUS: *Esah einai el heharim, mei-ayin yavo ezri?*
Ezri mei-im Adonai, oseih shamayim vaaretz.

I lift my eyes up to the sun
Where on earth will my help come from?
Come from heaven, come from earth,
Come from death and come from rebirth. (2x)

Chorus

There's blessing all around from the sky to the ground
So back down from your frown
Listen for the sound
If you're lost, stay put—just wait to be found
Plant yourself down

If you fall get up 'cause you're not that far gone
There's a new light about to shine into Zion
If you made it this far you can push through to dawn
Come on come on come on come on

I lift my eyes
I lift my eyes
To my surprise
To my surprise
Beneath the lies
Beneath the lies
I can rise and you can rise!

I can rise and you can rise
I can rise and you can rise
I can rise and you can rise
We can rise
We can rise
We can rise.

Sacred Sources

The Book of Ecclesiastes, or Kohelet *in Hebrew, is attributed to King Solomon writing late in his life. In the introduction to his commentary on the book, Michael Fox writes that* Kohelet *"gives voice to an experience not usually thought of as religious: the pain and frustration engendered by an unblinking gaze at life's absurdities and injustices" (Michael V. Fox,* The JPS Bible Commentary: Ecclesiastes, *p. ix). Yet, even within this bleak view, there is hope that can inspire resilience. The author never gives up on his search for meaning in life, despite its unpredictability and challenge. Indeed, the book's point is that human wisdom is in knowing that no matter how wise one may be, there are no answers to the vagaries of life. Justice is delayed, the wicked may go unpunished, the good may suffer, and the deep questions of life are unfathomable. And yet,* Kohelet *advises us to make the best of our lives, finding pleasure where we can as we struggle through the work of our days. Ultimately, everything is in God's hands.*

> There is a frustration that occurs in the world: sometimes an upright person is requited according to the conduct of the scoundrel; and sometimes the scoundrel is requited according to the conduct of the upright. I say all that is frustration. I therefore praised enjoyment: For the only good a person can have under the sun is to eat and drink and enjoy themselves. That much can accompany a person in exchange for their wealth, through the days of life that God has granted us under the sun. (Ecclesiastes 8:14–17)

> The praise of enjoyment mentioned here is to teach you that the Divine Presence rests upon an individual neither from an atmosphere of sadness, nor from an atmosphere of laziness, nor from an atmosphere of laughter, nor from an atmosphere of frivolity, nor from an atmosphere of idle conversation, nor from an atmosphere of idle chatter, but rather from an atmosphere that is imbued with the joy of mitzvah. (Babylonian Talmud, *Shabbat* 30b)

- Where is the potential for joy in the midst of life's mysteries, absurdities, and pain?
- According to the Rabbinic text, where might we find the enjoyment *Kohelet* recommends?
- How might you apply this counsel to your own life?

Poetry and Prayer

What the Living Do

Marie Howe

Johnny, the kitchen sink has been clogged for days, some utensil probably fell down there.
And the Drano won't work but smells dangerous, and the crusty dishes have piled up

waiting for the plumber I still haven't called. This is the everyday we spoke of.
It's winter again: the sky's a deep, headstrong blue, and the sunlight pours through

the open living-room windows because the heat's on too high in here and I can't turn it off.
For weeks now, driving, or dropping a bag of groceries in the street, the bag breaking,

I've been thinking: This is what the living do. And yesterday, hurrying along those
wobbly bricks in the Cambridge sidewalk, spilling my coffee down my wrist and sleeve,

I thought it again, and again later, when buying a hairbrush: This is it.
Parking. Slamming the car door shut in the cold. What you called that yearning.

What you finally gave up. We want the spring to come and the winter to pass. We want
whoever to call or not call, a letter, a kiss—we want more and more and then more of it.

But there are moments, walking, when I catch a glimpse of myself in the window glass,
say, the window of the corner video store, and I'm gripped by a cherishing so deep

for my own blowing hair, chapped face, and unbuttoned coat that I'm speechless:
I am living. I remember you.

Psalm 126:3
The Eternal will do great things for us and we shall rejoice.

Kaddish and Mourning Prayers

See page 175.

Kaddish and Mourning Prayers

Mourner's Kaddish

Yitgadal v'yitkadash sh'meih raba	יִתְגַּדַּל וְיִתְקַדַּשׁ שְׁמֵהּ רַבָּא
b'alma di v'ra chiruteih,	בְּעָלְמָא דִּי בְרָא כִרְעוּתֵהּ,
v'yamlich malchuteih b'chayeichon	וְיַמְלִיךְ מַלְכוּתֵהּ בְּחַיֵּיכוֹן
uvyomeichon uvchayei d'chol beit	וּבְיוֹמֵיכוֹן וּבְחַיֵּי דְכָל בֵּית
Yisrael, baagala uvizman kariv,	יִשְׂרָאֵל, בַּעֲגָלָא וּבִזְמַן קָרִיב,
v'imru: amen.	וְאִמְרוּ: אָמֵן.
Y'hei sh'meih raba m'varach	יְהֵא שְׁמֵהּ רַבָּא מְבָרַךְ
l'alam ul'almei almaya.	לְעָלַם וּלְעָלְמֵי עָלְמַיָּא.
Yitbarach v'yishtabach, v'yitpaar	יִתְבָּרַךְ וְיִשְׁתַּבַּח, וְיִתְפָּאַר
v'yitromam v'yitnasei, v'yit'hadar	וְיִתְרוֹמַם וְיִתְנַשֵּׂא, וְיִתְהַדַּר
v'yit'aleh v'yit'halal sh'meih d'kudsha,	וְיִתְעַלֶּה וְיִתְהַלַּל שְׁמֵהּ דְּקֻדְשָׁא,
b'rich hu,	בְּרִיךְ הוּא,
l'eila min kol birchata v'shirata,	לְעֵֽלָּא מִן כָּל בִּרְכָתָא וְשִׁירָתָא,
tushb'chata v'nechemata daamiran	תֻּשְׁבְּחָתָא וְנֶחֱמָתָא דַּאֲמִירָן
b'alma, v'imru: amen.	בְּעָלְמָא, וְאִמְרוּ: אָמֵן.
Y'hei sh'lama raba min sh'maya	יְהֵא שְׁלָמָא רַבָּא מִן שְׁמַיָּא
v'chayim aleinu v'al kol Yisrael,	וְחַיִּים עָלֵינוּ וְעַל כָּל יִשְׂרָאֵל,
v'imru: amen.	וְאִמְרוּ: אָמֵן.
Oseh shalom bimromav, hu yaaseh	עֹשֶׂה שָׁלוֹם בִּמְרוֹמָיו, הוּא יַעֲשֶׂה
shalom aleinu v'al kol Yisrael,	שָׁלוֹם עָלֵינוּ וְעַל כָּל יִשְׂרָאֵל,
v'imru: amen.	וְאִמְרוּ: אָמֵן.

Exalted and hallowed be God's great name
In the world which God created, according to plan.
May God's majesty be revealed in the days of our lifetime
And the life of all Israel— speedily, imminently,
To which we say Amen.
Blessed be God's great name to all eternity.

Blessed, praised, honored, exalted, extolled, glorified, adored, and lauded be the name of the Holy Blessed One, beyond all earthly words and songs of blessing, praise, and comfort,
To which we say Amen.
May there be abundant peace from heaven, and life, for us and all Israel.
To which we say Amen.
May the One who creates harmony on high bring peace to us and to all Israel.
To which we say Amen.

Mourning Prayer

Music: Anita Schubert

SING:

זִכְרוֹנוֹ לִבְרָכָה, זִכְרוֹנָהּ לִבְרָכָה, זִכְרוֹנָם לִבְרָכָה.

Zichrono livrachah, zichronah livrachah, zichronam livrachah.

May his memory be for a blessing, may her memory be for a blessing, may their memory be for a blessing.
We are blessed remembering you.

Resources

Alter, Robert. *The Book of Psalms*. New York: Norton, 2007.

Brenner, Anne. *Mourning and Mitzvah: A Guided Journal for Walking the Mourner's Path Through Grief to Healing*, rev. ed. Woodstock, VT: Jewish Lights Press, 2017.

Cowan, Rachel and Linda Thal. *Wise Aging: Living With Joy, Resilience, and Spirit.* Springfield, NJ: Behrman House, 2015.

Diamant, Anita. *Saying Kaddish: How to Comfort the Dying, Bury the Dead, and Mourn as a Jew.* New York: Schocken, 2007.

Eisner, Elliot. *The Educational Imagination.* New York: Macmillan, 1979.

Fox, Michael V. *The JPS Bible Commentary: Ecclesiastes*. Philadelphia: Jewish Publication Society, 2004.

Friedman, Dayle. *Jewish End of Life Care in a Virtual Age*. Albion Andalus Books, 2021.

Glick, Shmuel. *Light and Consolation: The Development of Jewish Consolation Practices.* Trans. Fern Seckbach. Jerusalem: Schocken Institute for Jewish Research of the Jewish Theological Seminary of America, 2004.

Hirsch, Richard. *The Journey of Mourning*. Wyncote, PA: Reconstructionist Rabbinical College Press, 2006.

Hoffman, Lawrence A., ed. *Traditional Prayers, Modern Commentaries*, Vol. 6. Woodstock, VT: Jewish Lights, 2002.

Katz, Marc. *The Heart of Loneliness: How Jewish Wisdom Can Help You Cope and Find Comfort*. Woodstock, VT: Jewish Lights Press, 2016.

Kessler, David. www.grief.com.

Klein, Isaac and Joel Roth. *A Guide to Jewish Religious Practice.* New York: Jewish Theological Seminary of America, 1992.

Lamm, Maurice. *Consolation: The Spiritual Journey Beyond Grief.* Philadelphia: Jewish Publication Society, 2004.

Matlins, Stuart, editor. *The Jewish Book of Grief and Healing: A Spiritual Companion for Mourning.* Woodstock, VT: Jewish Lights Press, 2016.

Olitzky, Kerry. *Grief in Our Seasons: A Mourner's Kaddish Companion.* Woodstock, VT: Jewish Lights Press, 1998.

Sources and Permissions

The Central Conference of American Rabbis expresses gratitude to the publishers and writers for permissions we have received to reprint their material in this book. Every effort has been made to ascertain the proper owners of copyrights for the selections used in this volume and to obtain permission to reprint copyrighted content where required. CCAR Press will be pleased, in subsequent editions, to correct any inadvertent errors or omissions that may be pointed out.

Torah translations are taken from *The Torah: A Modern Commentary*, revised edition (New York: CCAR Press, 2005), edited by Rabbi W. Gunther Plaut. Translations of Psalms are from *Songs Ascending: The Book of Psalms in a New Translation with Textual and Spiritual Commentary* by Rabbi Richard N. Levy (New York: CCAR Press, 2018). Talmud translations are adapted from *The William Davidson Talmud*, available on sefaria.org.

ix Lawrence A. Hoffman, *The Art of Public Prayer: Not for Clergy Only* (Woodstock, VT: Jewish Lights Publishing, 1999), 17.

ix Kenneth I. Pargament, *Spiritually Integrated Psychotherapy: Understanding and Addressing the Sacred* (New York: Guilford Press, 2011), 81.

x H. Rafael Goldstein and J.B. Sacks, *Psalms in the Key of Healing: A Text Study for Clergy, Chaplains, and People Living with Illness*, ed. (Boulder, CO: Albion-Andalus Books, 2021), 82.

xi Mitch Albom, *Tuesdays with Morrie: An Old Man, a Young Man, and Life's Greatest Lesson* (New York: Anchor Books, 2006), 174.

xi Daniel Gottlieb, *The Wisdom We're Born With: Restoring Our Faith in Ourselves* (New York: Sterling Ethos, 2014), 87.

4 Alden Solovy, "In Sorrow," in *Mishkan Aveilut: Where Grief Resides*, ed. Rabbi Eric Weiss (New York: CCAR Press, 2019), 119. Used by permission.

7 Nancy Schaffer, "Because We Spill Not Only Milk" in *Instructions in Joy: Meditations* (Boston: Skinner House Books, 2002). Used by permission.

10 Rivka Miriam, "Tearing," trans. Steven Sager. Available online at https://sichaconversation.files.wordpress.com/2015/02/tearing-and-repairing-binder-hevra-kaddisha-2016.pdf.

13 Karyn D. Kedar, "The Valley," in *Amen: Seeking Presence with Prayer, Poetry,*

and Mindfulness Practice (New York: CCAR Press, 2020), 108. Used by permission.

15 Karyn D. Kedar, "To the God, Who Teaches," in *Amen: Seeking Presence with Prayer, Poetry, and Mindfulness Practice* (New York: CCAR Press, 2020), 95–96. Used by permission.

18 Yehuda Amichai, "From Songs of Zion the Beautiful: 34" in *The Selected Poetry of Yehuda Amichai*, edited and translated from the Hebrew by Chana Bloch and Stephen Mitchell. © 1986, 1996, 2013 by Chana Bloch and Stephen Mitchell. Published by the University of California Press. Used by permission.

20 Eric Weiss, "Loss-Change," from *Mishkan Aveilut: Where Grief Resides*, ed. Eric Weiss (New York: CCAR Press, 2019), 10. Used by permission.

23, 28 "*Ratzo VaShov* (Ebb and Flow)," English lyrics and music by Cantor Lisa B. Segal © 2017. Based on Ezekiel 1:14. Previously published in the songbook *Kol Isha: Songs and Settings of Prayers* (2019) from members of the Women Cantors Network.

24 Joy Ladin, "Lost and Found," from *The Future is Trying to Tell Us Something: New and Selected Poems* (Rhinebeck, NY: Sheep Meadow, 2017). Used by permission of the author.

25, 34 "*Esa Chanfei Shachar*," English lyrics and music © 2002 Abby Bernstein Gostein. All rights reserved. abbygostein.com.

26 Luci Shaw, "Revival," from *What the Light Was Like* (Seattle: WordFarm, 2006), 68. © 2006 by Luci Shaw. Used by permission of the publisher (www.wordfarm.net).

29 Carl Sandburg, "Under the Harvest Moon," from *Chicago Poems* (New York: Henry Holt and Company, 1916), 116.

31, 36 "Lamdeini," text by Leah Goldberg, translated by Pnina Peli. Music by Benjie Ellen Schiller, recorded on *A World Fulfilled* © 2002. Music published by Transcontinental Music.

32 Lawrence A. Hoffman, *The Journey Home: Discovering the Spiritual Wisdom of the Jewish Tradition* (Boston, MA: Beacon Press, 2002), 160, 171.

32 Victoria Safford, "Hope," from *Walking Toward Morning* (Boston: Skinner House Books, 2003). Used by permission.

34 "A Psalm of Found Joy: For the First Joy in Months" by Devon A. Spier, rabbinical student. First published on Ritualwell.org. Used by permission.

38 Andrea Hollander Budy, "For Weeks after the Funeral" from *Woman in the Painting*. © 2006 by Andrea Hollander Budy. Reprinted with the permission of The Permissions Company, LLC on behalf of Autumn House, autumnhouse.org.

39 "*Eil Na R'fa Na Lah*," © 2017, from the album *Mikolot Mayim* by Feliza and Or Zohar. Music by Or Zohar, lyrics arranged by Or Zohar, based on the

Book of Numbers, the Serenity prayer, and a traditional Jewish prayer for healing. Recorded by Feliza and Or Zohar.

41 "Everything That Was Broken" by Mary Oliver. Reprinted by the permission of The Charlotte Sheedy Literary Agency as agent for the author. © NW Orchard LLC 2015 with permission by Bill Reichblum.

46 Linda Pastan, "The Five Stages of Grief," in *The Five Stages of Grief: Poems* (New York, W.W. Norton & Company, 1978). © 1978 by Linda Pastan. Used by permission of W.W. Norton & Company, Inc.

50 Rolf Jacobsen, "Just Delicate Needles," in *The Roads Have Come to an End Now: Selected and Last Poems of Rolf Jacobsen*, trans. Robert Bly, Roger Greenwald and Robert Hedin (Port Townsend, WA: Copper Canyon Press, 2001), 138–139. Used by permission of Robert Hedin.

52 Daniel Polish, *Bringing the Psalms to Life: How to Understand and Use the Book of Psalms*. (Woodstock, VT: Jewish Lights Publishing, 2000), xii-xiii.

53 Hilda Yael Kessler, "Uncharted Territory." © Hilda Yael Kessler, reprinted with permission of Chanan Kessler. This and other writings by Hilda appeared in the memory book "Messages."

56 Zelda, "Don't Distance Yourself," trans. Steven Sager. Available online at https://sichaconversation.files.wordpress.com/2015/02/the-work-of-carring-and-caring2015.pdf

58 From "In My Life, On My Life" from *Open Closed Open* by Yehuda Amichai. Compilation © 2000 by Yehuda Amichai. © by Chana Bloch and Chana Kronfeld. Used by permission of HarperCollins Publishers, Georges Borchardt, Inc., and Hana Amichai.

60 Deborah Greene, "Grief in Haiku." Available online on her blog, *Reflecting Out Loud*, at https://reflectingoutloud.net/2016/01/22/grief-in-haiku/. Used by permission.

63 Pamela Wax, "Dropping Stones from the Heart (with chest-pounding)." © Pamela Wax. Used by permission.

67, 73 "*Asher Yatzar*," English lyrics and music © 2016 Dan Nichols.

68 Alden Solovy, "Meditation on Mitzvot," in *This Joyous Soul: A New Voice for Ancient Yearnings* (New York: CCAR Press, 2019), 18. Used by permission.

70 Harold S. Kushner, *When Bad Things Happen to Good People* (New York: Anchor Books, 2004), 133.

71 Jane Kenyon, "Let Evening Come" from *Collected Poems*. Copyright © 2005 by The Estate of Jane Kenyon. Reprinted with the permission of The Permissions Company, LLC on behalf of Graywolf Press, Minneapolis, MN, graywolfpress.org.

73 Harold S. Kushner, *When Bad Things Happen to Good People* (New York: Anchor Books, 2004), 133.

74 "Mourning to Dancing" by Devon A. Spier, rabbinical student. First published on Ritualwell.org. Used by permission.

77 Alden Solovy, "Your Name: Meditation at Dusk," in *This Grateful Heart: Psalms and Prayers for a New Day* (New York: CCAR Press, 2017), 11. Used by permission.

78 Harold S. Kushner, *When Bad Things Happen to Good People* (New York: Anchor Books, 2004), 138.

78, 83 "*Nachamu*," English lyrics and music © 2018 Elana Arian. All rights reserved.

79 Rabbi Abraham Joshua Heschel, "Prayer Invites," in *Mishkan T'filah for the House of Mourning* (New York: CCAR Press, 2010), 15b. Used by permission of Prof. Susannah Heschel.

81 Dara Horn, *The World to Come* (New York: Norton, 2006), 124.

82 Karyn D. Kedar, "The Archaeologist of the Soul," in *Amen: Seeking Presence with Prayer, Poetry, and Mindfulness Practice* (New York: CCAR Press, 2020), 13–14. Used by permission.

84 *Shekhinah [God's Presence] does not reside*, Elijah de Vidas in *Safed Spirituality: Rules of Mystical Piety, the Beginning of Wisdom*, trans. Lawrence Fine (Mahwah, NJ: Paulist Press, 1984).

88 Dave Yedid, "We Have Always Been," in *Mishkan Ga'avah: Where Pride Dwells*, ed. Denise L. Eger (New York: CCAR Press, 2020), 152. Used by permission.

90 Roberta Temes, *Living with an Empty Chair: A Guide through Grief* (Far Hills, NJ: New Horizon Press, 1992), 93.

90, 103 "*Olam Chesed Yibaneh*," English lyrics and music © 2002 Rabbi Menachem Creditor.

91 Joy Ladin, "Comfort Animal," from *Shekhinah Speaks* (Chicago: Selva Oscura Press, 2022). Used by permission of the author.

91 Edith Sitwell, "Eurydice," from *Collected Poems of Edith Sitwell*, ed. Edith Sitwell and Osbert Sitwell (New York: Vanguard Press, 1968), 263.

94 Harold S. Kushner, *When Bad Things Happen to Good People* (New York: Anchor Books, 2004), 149.

95 Trisha Arlin, "A Mourner's *Kaddish*." © 2013 by Trisha Arlin. Available online at http://triganza.blogspot.com/2013/12/a-mourners-kadish.html. Used by permission.

99 "On your journey you will come" by Muriel Rukeyser in *The Collected Poems of Muriel Rukeyser*. © 2005 by Muriel Rukeyser. Reprinted by permission of ICM Partners.

102 Lisel Mueller, "Hope," from *Alive Together* (Baton Rouge: Louisiana State University Press, 1996), 103. Used by permission.

104 Harold M. Schulweis, "Life and Death," *From Prose to Poetry* (Encino, CA: The Schulweis Institute, 2015), 151. Used by permission.

106 Richard Levy, "Reflection Before Kaddish," in *Mishkan T'filah: A Reform Siddur*, ed. Elyse D. Frishman (New York: CCAR Press, 2007), 597.

109, 115 "Those Who Sow," music and lyrics by Debbie Friedman. Copyright © 2013 by the Farf, Inc. International copyright secured. All rights reserved.

110 Stuart Kestenbaum, "Prayer for the Dead," from *Prayers & Run-on Sentences* (Cumberland, ME: Deerbrook Editions, 2007), 25. Used by permission.

113 Barbara Leff, "Stones (At Normandy)," in *Mishkan Aveilut: Where Grief Resides*, ed. Eric Weiss (New York: CCAR Press, 2019), 96–97.

116 Rumi, "Birdwings," in *The Essential Rumi*, trans. Coleman Barks (New York: HarperOne, 2004), 174.

119 Judith Plaskow, "Wrestling with God and Evil," in *Goddess and God in the World: Conversations in Embodied Theology* by Carol P. Christ and Judith Plaskow (Minneapolis, MN: Fortress Press, 2016), 118–189.

120 E.E. Cummings, "i thank You God for most this amazing" from *Selected Poems*, introduction and commentary by Richard S. Kennedy. ©1950, 1978, 1991 by the Trustees for the E. E. Cummings Trust. © 1979 by George James Firmage. Used by permission of Liveright Publishing Corporation.

122 Alden Solovy, "Soul Shine," in *This Joyous Soul: A New Voice for Ancient Yearnings* (New York: CCAR Press, 2019), 130. Used by permission.

125 Chana Bloch, "Afterlife," in *The Past Keeps Changing* (Rhinebeck, NY: Sheep Meadow, 1992).

124 Arthur Green, *Seek My Face: A Jewish Mystical Theology* (Northvale, NJ: Jason Aronson, 2003), 175.

127 Dorianne Laux, "Dust" from *What We Carry*. © 1994 by Dorianne Laux. Reprinted the permission of The Permissions Company, LLC on behalf of BOA Editions, Ltd., boaeditions.org.

132 "By the Well of Living and Seeing: 36" from *The Poems of Charles Reznikoff: 1918-1975*, edited by Seamus Cooney. © 1969 by Charles Reznikoff. © 2005 by The Estate of Charles Reznikoff. Reprinted by permission of The Permissions Company, LLC on behalf of Black Sparrow/David R Godine, Publisher, Inc., godine.com.

132 E.E. Dessler, *Strive for Truth: Michtav Me-Eliyahu: The Selected Writings of E. E. Dessler*, trans. Aryeh Carmell, vol. 2 (Nanuet, NY: Feldheim Publishers, 1978), 56–57.

134 Debra Cash, "Mourner's Kaddish for Everyday," in *Mishkan Aveilut: Where*

Grief Resides, ed. Rabbi Eric Weiss (New York: CCAR Press, 2019), 125. © by Debra Cash. All rights reserved. Used by permission of the author.

135, 141 "We Are Loved," lyrics © Rabbi Rami Shapiro, music © 2015 Shir Yaakov Feit (Shiryaakov.com).

137 Martin Rawlings-Fein, "The Righteous" excerpted from "The Westward Amidah," in *Mishkan Ga'avah: Where Pride Dwells*, ed. Rabbi Denise L. Eger (New York: CCAR Press, 2020), 27. First published on Ritualwell.org. © 2020 by Martin Rawlings-Fein. Used by permission.

138 Adapted from "We Remember Them" by Rabbi Sylvan Kamens and Rabbi Jack Riemer in *Gates of Prayer: The New Union Prayer Book* (New York: CCAR Press, 1975), 552. Music by Rabbi Ken Chasen and Rabbi Yoshi Zweiback. © 2018 Chase Avenue Music (BMI).

139 Wisława Szymborska, "Cat in an Empty Apartment," in *Poems New and Collected: 1957-1997*, trans. Stanisław Barańczak and Clare Cavanagh (New York: Houghton Mifflin Harcourt, 1998), 238.

139 Elisabeth Kübler-Ross and David Kessler, *On Grief and Grieving: Finding the Meaning of Grief through the Five Stages of Loss* (New York: Scribner, 2005), 230.

141 Harold S. Kushner, *When Bad Things Happen to Good People* (New York: Anchor Books, 2004), 87.

142 *So what is there to say*, Jane Vonnegut Yarmolinsky, *Angels Without Wings* (New York: Houghton Mifflin Harcourt, 1987), 264.

145 David White, "Just Beyond Yourself," in *The Bell and the Blackbird*, © Many Rivers Press, Langley, WA. Reprinted by permission of Many Rivers Press, www.davidwhyte.com.

148 Mary Elizabeth Frye, traditional attribution, "Do Not Stand at My Grave and Weep."

155 Abraham E. Millgram, *Jewish Worship* (Philadelphia: Jewish Publication Society, 1971), 33.

156 Rachel Barenblat, "Seven Stops." © 2015 Rachel Barenblat. Available online at https://velveteenrabbi.blogs.com/blog/2015/05/day-31-of-the-omer.html. Used by permission.

162 Karyn D. Kedar, "*Kaddish*: You Ask So Much," in *Amen: Seeking Presence with Prayer, Poetry, and Mindfulness Practice* (New York: CCAR Press, 2020), 105. Used by permission.

163 "Each of Us Has a Name," text by Zelda and English translation by Marcia Lee Falk. Music composed by Hanan Yuval and sung by Chava Alberstein.

166 Lewis John Eron, "When Will I Be Myself Again," in *Mishkan Aveilut:*

Where Grief Resides, ed. Eric Weiss (New York: CCAR Press, 2019), 23. © Lewis John Eron. Used by permission.

168 *It is customary for Jews*, Zoë Klein. Used by permission.

171 "We Can Rise" from the album *We Can Rise*. English text and music by Chana Rothman (chanarothmanmusic.com). © Chana Rothman 2007 ASCAP.

173 Marie Howe, "What the Living Do", from *What the Living Do*. © 1997 by Marie Howe. Used by permission of W. W. Norton & Company, Inc.

About the Editors

Rabbi Lisa D. Grant, PhD, is Director of the New York Rabbinical School program, Eleanor Sinsheimer Distinguished Service Professor in Jewish Education, and Coordinator of Special Seminary projects at the Hebrew Union College–Jewish Institute of Religion. In addition to authoring numerous articles, book chapters, and curriculum guides, she is coauthor with Ezra Kopelowitz of *Israel Education Matters: A 21st Century Paradigm for Jewish Education*. She is coeditor of *International Handbook of Jewish Education* with Helena Miller and Alex Pomson, and with Diane T. Schuster, Meredith Woocher, and Steven M. Cohen, author of *A Journey of Heart and Mind: Transformative Jewish Learning in Adulthood*.

Rabbi Grant has been on the faculty of HUC-JIR since 2000. She received her BA from the University of Michigan, Ann Arbor, an MBA from the University of Massachusetts, Amherst, a PhD from the Jewish Theological Seminary in New York, and rabbinic ordination from Hebrew Union College–Jewish Institute of Religion. She is happily married to Billy Weitzer and the proud mother of two adult children.

Cantor Lisa B. Segal serves as cantor and is a founding member of congregation Kolot Chayeinu/Voices of Our Lives in Park Slope, Brooklyn. Ordained in 2011 by the Academy for Jewish Religion in New York, she served as their Director of Cantorial Studies from 2012 to 2014. With her unique voice and spirit, Cantor Segal composes music, creates and leads ritual, and performs in concert, online, and on bimahs beyond her synagogue. Cantor Segal is a member of the American Conference of Cantors. She and her husband, writer and *maggid* Arthur "Ari" Strimling, live in Park Slope.

NOTES

NOTES

NOTES

NOTES

NOTES